Dennis -
HAPPY
HAUNTINGS!

My Home Is Haunted...
Now What?!

By Barry FitzGerald and Dustin J. Pari

Dedication

We would like to dedicate this book to all the people that took time out of their busy lives to contribute to this publication. Without them it would not have been completed and we are truly grateful. Of course we would also like to include those representatives of different belief systems and cultures that added their knowledge bringing this book full circle, their generosity and kindness will always be fondly remembered.

But we also would like to include in this dedication all those souls that have been forgotten over time. Those spirits that cry for attention and help, without their effect on our lives this book would not have come into being and for this we thank you and in our own uncomplicated way, *'we remember you.'*

"NOW GO AWAY AND LEAVE US ALONE :) "

Barry FitzGerald.

Acknowledgements

Barry would like to thank once again the support of family, friends and fans for their support whilst we collected the information expressed in this publication. Tearah for her wonderful poem, Terri J Garafalo from Entities-R-Us for the artwork and Ryan Ball for his editing skills and I cannot forget Brette Miller for her patients in creating a fantastic cover. Thank you all.

Of course I cannot forget the spirits that gave of their self to supply experiences and people which resulted in one of the greatest paper trails I have ever known.

Dustin's support has once again proved a corner stone in this project and his friendship and laughter made the journey much shorter and as the end of day comes closer we simply raise a glass to the setting sun in thanks.

Barry FitzGerald.

I would like to thank God every day for the blessings in my life that have been bestowed upon me, no matter how undeserving I might be. I aspire to enlighten others to God's presence in their lives so that they too may recognize the presence of the Holy Spirit in their lives.

It is with a full and thankful heart that I acknowledge all those who spoke with us and shared with us their beliefs, their stories, and their souls. The bond that binds us all in this life was never more apparent to me than during the writing of this book. No matter what language we speak, no matter what place we call home, we truly are all in this together.

Once again my hat is tipped to Mr. Barry FitzGerald who is not only a gentleman and a scholar, but also a dear friend and truly one of the most admirable souls my tired eyes have ever come across. It has been a pleasure to once again craft a work of such importance with you.

To Marc Tetlow whose advice and friendship has far exceeded that of anyone who I have had the pleasure to work with, I thank you for spending so much time listening to me and helping me stay focused.

To my parents who instilled in me a sense of purpose and honesty, and also taught me that this life isn't solely about us, but that we must constantly be aware of the needs of those around us, in our family, in our community and in our world.

To my sweet little wife Diane who is a constant source of sweet love and inspiration- nothing I have done these past few years could have been remotely possible without your constant support, understanding, sacrifice and chicken cutlets. You will always be my one and only- you sexy little vixen.

To our boys Nathan and Jake whom make me increasingly proud as the days go on, I thank you for being who you are, for being true to yourselves, for being respectful of your mother and loving to your sister. You may never know how much you both mean to me.

To my daughter known most affectionately as "Beans", Daddy loves you with all his heart and always will, in this life and beyond. You are the embodiment of all that is right, beautiful and worth loving in this world. You are innocence and joy, you are sunshine and warmth, and in short- you are the reason Daddy gets up in the morning.

May the Angels of the Lord always surround you and protect you from the evils of this world and the next, both the seen and the unseen. And above all else, always, always know that you are loved and that every sacrifice I have ever made was for the betterment of you and our family and for nothing else.

Dustin Pari

Table of Contents

This book has been designed and written by
researchers for researchers.

Introduction

A word from Barry

The following pages should not be taken lightly, many people who use the techniques disclosed in these pages have been professionals working in the grey area of paranormal research and spirituality for a long time and know the entities they pitch themselves against.
But it was of great importance to both Dustin and I to once again take another look at the paranormal and analyze it a little further like we did with our last publication, 'The Complete Approach'.

So your house is haunted, what can you do, or who can you turn to for help? This publication looks at a wide range of ideas which may offer a solution to your haunted home collected from around the world. But we took it a little further instead of telling you which techniques will work and those that will not, we have explored it in greater detail to tell you why they work and more about the faith and belief system of the people that claim it.

So many people have approached me asking what can I do? A team has gone into your home, you suspect it to be haunted and then they confirm it and leave you holding the torch. What's next?

This book gives you the homeowner the details

required to make an informed decision on your next step. The
information has been collected from all over the world and from varying belief systems.

You are your own judge and counsel in regards the information bestowed to you in this book. Find what works for you and take control of a situation which has left many fearful of their next bedtime phantom experience, fearful for the safety of their children, take control.

A word from Dustin

Over the years I have been approached by so many people from all walks of life, asking what they should do in regards to paranormal activity within their own home.

As someone who has traveled the Earth and has come face to face with various entities in numerous encounters, I can completely understand the importance of finding a solution to something that can be very frightening for many people caught unawares.
It is in this spirit that Barry and I present this publication, designed to help people of various belief systems found the world over.

We have thoroughly interviewed men and women from different religions, societies and backgrounds that we have come across in our travels. We have walked with them and talked with them, we have studied their faiths and

submerged ourselves in their various cultures, all to gain a more insightful understanding as to how each individual both views the phenomenon of paranormal activity and most importantly, how they deal with it.

It is our wish that within the pages of this book, you the reader will not only share in a vast understanding of the paranormal field, but that you will also find the insight necessary to help yourself and others as we all walk this dark and mysterious road together.

Knowledge is the key.

Chapter 1
A Hauntingly Brief Overview

"Death is not the end."
Ambrose Bierce

So your house is haunted…now what?!

To say it is unnerving to live in a house with some types of paranormal activity is to put it mildly? Not knowing what to expect, not being able to feel at ease in your own bed chambers, always wondering if there is something or someone lurking just beyond, hiding in the shadows, watching and waiting- this is enough to turn even the most hardnosed skeptic into a believer and perhaps even result in an undisclosed sale of the property itself.

For many people the world over, there may come a time where their dream home becomes an absolute nightmare.

So why do these things happen? Why is there sometimes a sudden and drastic change in the spiritual atmosphere of a dwelling? What exactly is happening? And of course- what can you do about it?

These are the questions that we are aiming to answer in this publication.

By systematically going through the numerous interviews collected we are confident that you will find the answers that you need within the pages of this publication.
But before we delve into the world of spiritual cleansings, blessings, talismans and various other

ways to ward off and banish the things of the night, let us take a moment to review the different categories of haunting's as they are commonly known, but first there is one aspect which should be addressed and can be a very tricky matter to address; for those research groups dealing with a case where the client expresses signs of an over-active imagination.

Imagination:

This has to be the most troublesome of all non-threatening haunting's. An over active imagination can destroy a person's reasoning power and can speedily corrupt the susceptible minds of those friends and family members around them causing a snowball effect where every knock, bang and pop turns into a paranormal occurrence with damaging side effects and disturbed sleep patterns.

With sleep disrupted the over active imagination will continue to distract the deducing power of a normal mind. Studies have shown hallucinations can occur when emotional, or physical factors such as stress and extreme fatigue are involved causing the mechanism within the brain that helps to distinguish conscious perceptions and memory-based perceptions to misfire.
As a result, hallucinations occur during periods whilst you are awake. But the research team should note that an intelligent or non human can disguise

itself in non activity and simply make the onlooker quickly rule on a case of over-active imagination.

But this box should not be ticked to soon as it may take time to uncover the charlatan in its true form as many don't want to be discovered so their plans cannot be thwarted. So moving on once it has been confirmed your property is haunted we shall briefly explore the various types of haunting in their categories.

These following descriptions are a broad introduction to the phenomenon which is huge as inside each group there will be varying differences, but for the most part they will fit somewhere into each category.

Poltergeist Haunting:

Like most poltergeist cases the spontaneous nature of the phenomenon can be hard to track down as the activity can appear and disappear just as rapidly.
This type of phenomenon usually requires an agent and this can be found in the form of a young female or a teenage boy going through the stages of puberty, or just as likely from a person suffering extreme mental stress.

PK or Psycho kinesis is the movement of objects by oneself without his or her knowledge of it happening and completely by the power of the mind. In one familiar case I was aware of knives that levitated from a drawer in the subjects kitchen and stabbed her in the leg which and as you can imagine would be alarming to witness never mind experience.

PK is not the only answer to poltergeist phenomenon, Intelligent Spirits and In-humans are both able to manipulate objects. Some reports suggest the phenomenon happens progressively, increasing in its ruthlessness as it continues and typically falls dormant for a period of time after manifestation as the energy is expelled and needs time to revitalize. Phenomenon previously reported with in this research field include, random fires, bangs, objects being moved sometimes with great force, interference in electrical equipment and physical abuse and strange odours.

An unusual poltergeist case was reported in the 1960's in the West Yorkshire town of Pontefract in the UK and became known as 'The Pontefract Poltergeist'.

The house was rented by the Pritchard Family, Joe and Jean and their son Phil who was 15 years old and Diane who was their twelve year old daughter. The initial phenomenon started around 1966 and included the tell tale signs such as noises, smells and the appearance of pools of water which could not be explained by the authorities. But as witnessed with other similar cases the possible agent soon became the target as Diane suffered from various phenomenon including being thrown around her bedroom and dragged up the stairs.

Even after seeking advice and comfort from the Church the activity continued. On completion of the exorcism within
the property it was alleged a candle stick holder lifted off the mantle and hovered in full view and in front of the face of the Church representative.

Residual Haunting:

The more common haunting is known as a 'Residual' and simply are a shadow of the past, like a movie playing again and again over the course of time. They tend to occur in the same place and by definition are reoccurring events.
These echoes of individuals will not acknowledge the presence of people observing the phenomenon in present time, nor are they confined by the current placement of objects. They will appear to walk through walls, following a path from the past when such walls may not have existed.

Take for example the story of an electrician working in a basement in England, minding his own business as a legion
of Roman soldiers marched through the wall and across the basement and into the opposite wall. I

can only imagine the underwear clean up required after such an episode. But what he thought was curious was the legs below the knees were missing with all of them, but he was able to take note of the uniform which has since been verified as one of the Roman units serving in England almost 1000 years ago. Further excavation in the basement uncovered the mystery as the house was built over an old Roman Road and as it was several feet under the current basement level would explain why the legs were missing due to differences in floor levels. The roads were built by the soldiers and slaves to allow faster deployment of military units across England and were seen as quite revolutionary for its time, especially in England.

There is no real spirit only the impression and the scene is usually charged by environmental factors, stuck in this time loop playing over and over and therefore no communication can exist with a residual as there is no intelligence and it takes a good investigator to be able to distinguish between residual and the intelligent haunting's.

Intelligent Haunting:

"Intelligent" simply refers to the spirit possessing the ability to interrelate with us in some form or another.
In comparison to the Residual haunting, Intelligent Spirits are able to converse through various means

such as disembodied voices, Electrical Voice Phenomena (EVP) recording and object exploitation.

In the cases concerning manifestation the spirit can interact on occasions with the eyewitness and can be a positively
memorable experience or by the same token horrific in some cases depending on the personality of the spirit.

Take for instance the case Barry was involved with in County Donegal in Ireland. The house was reported to be haunted by a man in a huge hat and only appeared when an unmarried couple shared the same bed and was seen as an omen to a new child arriving, but was a frightening experience for all involved.

The house was closed for winter but the family gave him the keys and he went to investigate. On opening the door he smelt a sweet aroma, like flowers and is usually believed to be a positive sign of the nature of the haunting as within Christianity it was seen as a sign of angels and saints.

Further investigation uncovered it was not a man at all, but was a woman. The subject was a friend of the family who liked to come and visit and sit looking over the bay in silence. She was a nun.

It was a not a man in a top hat, it was this nun in a habit and she was letting the couples know of her disapproval of such sexual activities outside of marriage, which usually resulted in a child being conceived.

Barry left the nun to enjoy her new found home in peace and to govern the household in moral affairs as she saw fit.

But humans are not the only living things to come back to their beloved homes and loved ones; it's also a common occurrence for household pets to make their appearance. Cats and dogs are witnessed repeatedly for a time after their death, walking inside the house or sitting on a favorite chair, but these entities usually pass with time and strangely don't tend to be as approachable as they were when alive.

In-human

Probably the most dangerous type of a haunting you can run into and less known is that of the negative Inhuman. Differing from the other spirits as it is commonly believed was never alive in the sense we understand life like you and I, In-humans are often linked to demonic possession and come in many forms, but for the most part are not seen unless they want to be seen, usually to invoke fear and a breakdown of your defenses.

But there are two edges to a sword and likewise there are positive influences found under the umbrella of Inhuman.

This also includes more irregular angelic interaction, which can be somewhat pleasurable in contrast to their negative relations within this family group.

During Barry's earlier days of research into these negative entities he was involved in a case on the English borders but was unaware just how dangerous it was moving into it. During the case many entities came forward and acknowledged that they were not responsible for the extreme physical abusive carried out on the client and this was the first and only time this ever occurred during a case.

The entities were evasive and the attacks came in from many areas and we lost the client to a destructive possession, found in the road in a pool of her own blood. Barry is still haunted by the phone call he received from the entity. If there was ever a case referring to 'Legion' for we are many, this was it.

Time Slips:

The following listing is a little more controversial as it is rare but still happens and is called by its nature as a *Time Slip (though usually interpreted to be a haunting by witnesses)*

These are very bizarre and cause us great interest and tend to be one off events. The slip phenomenon happens all over the world and usually entails the witness observing another person which can happen at any time of the day or night, objects such as furniture may also be seen around them that are not there in present day and the person/spirit reacts to your presence usually in shock.

What we speculate is happening is a slip in time, how this happens we simply don't know. But it seems a limited form of interaction is allowed to happen, as this portal is open. We're very interested to look into these cases, as they are quite rare and quite unusual.

We would hope to find an old recorded instance in which the spirit being described is in fact that of the current owner. Meaning that a home-owner from the past had seen and documented the viewing of an apparition, which is detailed enough to fit the description and likeness of the present day home-owner.

However as of this day we have only been able to record instances of those from the past.
In theory they see us in their time and we see them, though the phenomenon usually only lasts for a few moments it is an incredible one to behold as it appears the veil that separates us thins, and the two are in the same place, though years apart.

One of the most famous time slips that occurred happened in France in the European Union.

Two ladies Charlotte Anne Moberly and Eleanor Jourdain happened to be visiting Versailles. As they enjoyed a leisurely stroll through the Petit Trianon gardens during the summer of 1901.

No doubt chatting to each other and not paying attention to their direction they became lost. As they passed by a deserted farmhouse a very heavy feeling began to quash their otherwise jovial spirits.

This doom and gloom continued and they had some interaction with some people older period costume that remains a mystery to this day.

Eleanor on further research discovered they had visited Versailles on the anniversary of the sacking of the Tuileries in 1792, when Louis XVI and Marie Antoinette had witnessed the massacre of their Swiss Guards and had been imprisoned in the Hall of the Assembly. Was this key anniversary the key to the time slip, we can only guess.

Some think there are explanations to be made for this phenomenon through the evolution of String Theory, which can be a bit complex to understand.

But here is another simple way of looking at a theory in regards to Time Slips and this one involves food, Dustin's favorite subject.

Picture a loaf of bread- each slice of bread is a moment in time in which we exist- normally the slices are equidistant from each other and do not intersect, but what if someone grabbed the bread and squished it like an accordion? What if, just at some special magical instant, the slices get squished together ever so slightly, and two different times exist as one for mere moments? We see each other for that brief moment, and then when the pressure on the loaf is released, we go back to our own plain of existence and our own moment in time.

Of course we do not have these answers, but from what we have seen of these Time Slips, the theory is as good as any other, maybe even better since it involves food.

Chapter 2

Sharing your home with ghosts

*"Yesterday upon the stair, I met a man who wasn't there.
He wasn't there again today. I wish to God he'd go away. "*

William Hughes Mearns

Many parents have heard stories from their children that they witnessed people coming out from the wardrobe, from under the bed, or even out from the closet and our hearts break as we look into their eyes and know with assurance they seen something and we are helpless to offer them any sanctuary from this nightmare as we adults cannot see what our children have described and even if we could what can we do about it?

So we shine a light in the darkness, we pour them a glass of milk; we pat them on the head and sweetly send them back to bed. But what happens when you do start to see the things that your children have described?

Sharing your quarters with ghosts can be a very terrifying thought. Knowing there are apparitions appearing within the very walls of your home, coming and going as they please can make every flick of the light switch, every step in the basement, every turn around the corner a nerve rattling experience.

The following are actual accounts of homeowners who have experienced these types of occurrence, it was very real for them and as you read the accounts we hope you understand the mental and physical pressures they had to endure to become veterans of a haunting.

We have protected their identity and only use their initials.

MK gave our first story to us, and it looks at the aspect of a haunting from a mothers perspective. Her story reiterates the fact that we should not be quick to rule on a case and to understand exactly what it is we are dealing with.

The Medium Child and Friends

'It started when my husband and I bought a 30-year old track home in Northern California. Soon after we moved there with our three children the main thing we noticed was the constant sense of seeing movement out of the corners of our eyes and the feeling that someone was with us.

I would often stay up late in the front room working on the computer but I always had the feeling that someone was standing behind me and would swing around to see no one there. I was so convinced that we had a ghost that I bought a voice activated recorder and put it in the front room on a night that all the kids were away for the weekend to avoid contamination. The next day there was one short recording of a child's voice saying, "Sorry, not my fault." I put the tape away and soon just went on with life.

Activities started to increase after my daughter was born. We started having a lot of electrical anomalies that could not be explained. I threw out one alarm clock thinking it was old and not working properly but the new one also would

29

"reset" itself to go off at odd hours. The same thing happened with my son's alarm clock. Older TV's and VCR's all started breaking down at the same time.

When my husband bought a digital ceiling fan/light for our bedroom it would switch itself on with great regularity. I would wake up in the middle of the night cold only to find the fan was on.

When I would get up to the power board, it would show it was "off" and I actually had to turn it on in order to turn it off. Other times the ceiling light would go on in the middle of the night and wake me up and I would have to go turn it off. One day during winter, after taking the kids to school I came home and found the ceiling fan on so in utter frustration I said out loud,

Fine! Have the fan on if you want it on that bad!

Then I got in the shower. When I got out, the fan was on the highest speed and was actually shaking back and forth. At that time I figured we had more than one ghost and that this one had an attitude. As my baby daughter grew into a toddler who was starting to talk, she became the one who was affected the most and aware of the child ghost the most. She would have conversations with someone she called "the little boy" with great regularity.

This was also the time when I started smelling cigarettes around the house. We didn't smoke so I would look outside to see if it was coming in from outdoors but I never saw anyone. I also started waking up with the sense of heavy smoke and the feeling that I was suffocating. It was so real that I would run down the hall looking for the fire, but there never was one, but since I have asthma, I am really sensitive to smoke and would feel like I had to leave the room to breathe again.

The last straw for me was when a fire almost started in the kitchen. I had a portable TV/VCR in the kitchen plugged in and the cords were lying on the burners but I knew the stove was off because I had just checked it and had put my hand on the burners to make sure they were cold. Seconds later the burner went on full and was red and burning through the cord. This happened within seconds and sparks were flying. That's when I decided that this "ghost" was a jerk and dangerous, so the next day I kicked him out. Basically going room to room with a crucifix and prayers but I didn't send the child ghost away, only the adult. All electrical mishaps stopped at that time and the cigarette smoke went away.

I actually heard the little boy spirit on two occasions. One night while I was trying to sleep, I heard the bedroom door handle rattle and a boy's voice calling, "mom? mom?". I rushed to the door thinking it was my son and swung it open only to find a dark, empty hallway. Down the hall I saw the bathroom light on so I thought that was my child and he was the one calling but what I found was my son was hiding in the bathroom terrified. His bedroom was in the front of the house and he had to walk down the long hallway to get to the bathroom and while he was doing so, he heard footsteps right behind him so he ran into the bathroom in fear.

I became so used to this that I didn't pay much attention, that is, until the ghost asked for help. My daughter would wake up several times a week crying and I would get her and bring her into my bed with me. On this final night, when I went into her room, she was crying "I scared--he's crying" I asked her who was crying and she said "the boy". I brought her into the bed with me and she was in the middle and I was on the side facing her when I heard a child's voice directly behind me saying, "help me." That's when I realised that it was cruel of me not to have helped him to heaven and I flashed back on all the episodes we had been through since we'd moved there and it all began to come together. I told the boy that I would get him help and not to fear. He let Annika sleep quietly after that. The next day I contacted a psychic/medium that I knew and he said that the ghost was of a boy that died of smoke inhalation (hence me waking up and not being able to breathe) and that the angry man ghost had been his father and was responsible for the fire that killed the boy. He said the man was long gone so I was effective in getting rid of him. (I found out later from my step-daughter that she used to wake up to see a grainy-

black-and-white figure of a man floating in her room, she just was afraid to mention it until all this came out.) Anyway, the psychic talked the boy over to the other side but he said we may notice something happen the next night, and we did. The next night I had trouble sleeping because the air felt so electrically charged that my skin buzzed. In the middle of the night my step-daughter screamed and ran into our room. She said her bedroom door opened and shut all by itself. The other kid's doors were also opened so something did happen. But then he was gone and I felt the difference. I actually cried the next day because I felt a sense of loss. This was the first time that I realised that our hearts (spirit) can be aware of and love someone that your physical mind is not aware of.

But that is not the end . . .

Apparently my daughter is a medium who attracts ghosts. About a year after that, I started to notice that my daughter was having conversations, again, with some invisible source. She said it was a girl. Then she started having fights with her. I would hear her saying, "Stop it! It's my doll, not yours!"

One day I was doing laundry in the garage when she came out and said, "Mommy, the girl is messing with my video games! Go tell her to stop!" So I went into her bedroom with her and asked her to point out the girl to me. She pointed to the corner so I felt silly but I talked to the "corner" telling the girl to behave. But then things started to grow a little creepier over time.

The following week while I was cooking dinner, Annika (my daughter), came into the room with her toy necklaces and said, "The girl said she can't wear my necklaces because she's not alive anymore." She caught my attention with that because sheltered 4 year-olds don't even understand the concept of alive and dead.

A couple nights later I was folding clothes on my bed when Annika came in with a sad expression and while caressing her own dress she said "the little girl has blood all over her head and dress 'cause she got killed." I just stared at her and had a major flashback to The Sixth Sense when the poor little boy had to deal with such horrors on his own and I realised that my daughter may be doing the same. I sat with her and asked her where the girl was and she said she was at the park (down the street from us). I told her that if she saw the girl again that she had to tell her to go to heaven and she sighed and said, "I know mommy. She has to go home with her mommy and daddy."

A few days later my father was babysitting her and he was freaked out because he said she was playing kick ball with him in the back yard when suddenly she turned and started yelling at someone whom he couldn't see. He said that she was yelling, "go home with your mommy and daddy now! You have to go home!" Then he said she returned back to playing ball with him as if nothing had happened. The girl never returned.'

This next story was kindly given to us by CJ and is told from the perspective of the child; a harrowing tale of childhood trauma that need not to happen.

The Unwanted Visitor

'When I was a little girl from about the ages of 5-6 years old I had been seeing this form I can only describe as a 'shadow man' and this continued until I was about 19-20 years old. It started in my bedroom which was in the basement of my home, but it was not the only place I would see this shadowy figure, but it was the main area I would see him. I would estimate this figure was about 6 foot tall and I could never make out his face, but he wasn't very friendly at all.

When I first started seeing him I was being woken up by either a loud bang or something calling my name and every time I was woken I would see this dark figure, sometimes he would just stand there near my door to the room and there were times he would even touch me.

I remember one night when I was approximately 10 years old I woke up and I heard what I believed to be a growl and a low deep voice, when I opened my eyes he was standing there. I wasn't glad to see him because every time I did, something would happen and I would either be scratched, hit or something else, something always happened. I just sat there on my bed and stared at him I didn't know what to do even though I have dealt with him before, I just sat there scared shaking and begging, 'please don't hurt me'.

In one instance a few things were thrown off my shelf and I felt something had grabbed me at the moment and I couldn't move, I was so scared I started screaming and crying, I didn't know what to do, it continued for a few more moments before finally ceasing, but even though the phenomenon was over I couldn't move for some minutes later. I finally broke free from my torture and switched the bedroom light on and jumped out of bed and made a dash upstairs to my Dad's bedroom screaming and crying to him.

My Dad just figured I experienced a nightmare and took me back to my room, he looked around the room and assured me nothing was there and went back to bed, but I knew what I experienced it wasn't a dream.

This entity would continue to make his presence known over the years.

I was 13 years old and moved into another room in my home, I thought I wouldn't see this shadow figure anymore, I wouldn't have to deal with what I

called "his torture"such as the pushing, the grabbing, the scratching and everything else, and I was hoping that I would no
longer feel like I had some sort of mental issue since I was the only that seemed to see this shadow man, but I was wrong. A few years later this shadow man came back, I was 16 years old and as I sat on my bed getting ready to go to sleep I felt like something had grabbed me, I got up very fast and I thought "what the heck?!" I looked around and saw nothing, first thing to go through my mind was "please don't let it be the shadow man". So I shrugged it off and tried to get to sleep and again I was grabbed and this time I felt something had grabbed my bed covers, again I got back up this time not very happy and yelled "what the heck!" again I looked around and saw nothing, and went to sleep. Without warning I was woken by a loud bang but this time I couldn't move, something was holding me down and I could hear a voice, low dark voice and I knew this voice well, I began to get scared I tried to yell but nothing happened,

I tried to move nothing worked, then I saw that it was the shadow man, as I lay there helpless I could hear his voice I couldn't make out what was being said, but to me it wasn't a very pleasant sound giving me the impression it was angry about something, this went on for a few minutes and finally stopped after he had moved away, I couldn't *breathe and still couldn't move for a couple minutes after his disappearance.*

When I was 19 years old the scariest thing then happened to me, I never talked about any of my experiences because I felt no one would understand or they would think I was demonic or had some sort of mental issue. I was woken between 3-4am, I kept hearing someone call my name it was a man's voice, so I figured it was my Dad, I got up and called out " yes Daddy?" no answer my Dad's bedroom door was shut, I went in there and he was asleep, so I just shrugged it off, but on my way back to bed I heard the calling again and I began following it downstairs into my old bedroom which was converted into a chill out room when I want to escape the pressures of the day. As I opened the door I said "hello" but there was no answer, I reached for the light and was thrown to the ground from behind, hitting my head on the ground, I lay there scared to death, not knowing what was going to happen next. As I lay there in shock I saw him standing at the edge of the room, he just stood there and I was frightened beyond words, feeling like I should even fear for my very life. He never touched me but I stayed there for about 30mins to an hour in shock before rushing back to my room. I grabbed my Bible and began reading it and praying to God, I was so scared, whatever or whoever it was is not pleasant to say the least, he was angry for some reason, for a long time I slept with my lights on in

38

my bedroom then switched to a black light and now I can sleep in peace..... finally'.

Of course a haunting is not limited to housewives and children. As if modern teenagers have not enough pressures to go through with education and bodily changes if you add a haunting Into the mix things can become disastrous. Our next story comes from CM.

The Haunted Cabin

'I was 18, I was a senior in high school and my family and I had been living in this log cabin for about two years. I went through hell in this cabin and the worst part was my parents didn't believe me nor my siblings, my Mom and Dad wouldn't even discuss the situation when I brought it up.

I was asleep one night in June shortly after my birthday when I awoke to the sounds of someone rustling through papers in my room which sat on my desk. My brother had been known to need a CD or something and come to my room to get it them so I didn't think much of it.

I do remember the room was unusually dark there was no light in the room at all which was odd because there was a street light outside. Well I sat up and rubbed my eyes thinking they needed to adjust and said, "Joey, what could you possibly want?" I received no response, instead the sound stopped and I had that gut feeling like when a predator has just levelled in on its prey and I felt like my life was in danger instantly.

I sat up and screamed as I heard footsteps slowly moving across the hardwood floor toward me. My father hearing this flew down the hall and slammed the door open and turned on the light. There was nothing there. All I knew was that I was wide-awake and wanted out of that room.

Two weeks had passed before the next happening. I was at home alone in the afternoon as I often was after school. My brother and sister had band lessons till 7pm and my Mom and Dad worked till 7pm also.

I was sitting in the living room when I heard a man whispering. I couldn't make it out but I knew I heard it. In my mind I thought it might have been wind fitting through a tight spot under a window or around a door, as it was an old house. Then I very clearly heard, "All alone," I could never forget the chills that rushed through my body when I heard those words. I ran from the house and used my cell phone to call my mom to tell her I was going out to my boyfriend's home not daring to go back inside.

The next day I obviously had to come home. I remember being very uncomfortable, even while showering I felt watched constantly. It started to make me very irritable. I was lying in my room doing my homework that night when I swore I heard my sister come into the room and shut the door. I said "You need any help with your math?" I heard her say "nah", I got up and stretched and announced I was going to get some food and as I started to walk I saw the room was empty. I ran down the hall and said nothing to anyone about it.

After a while I started to get really jumpy and nervous as other small things would begin to manifest. I'd wake up knowing I heard someone talking and there would be no one there. Things would be misplaced. I started waking up with scratches and cuts on my legs and back. Twice I came home and there was this horrid odour in my room. I didn't think much of it since we had squirrels in the walls and I figured one had simply died, trapped in the wall.

I will never forget a night in January that year. I had recently bought a bunk bed, a queen bed on bottom and a twin on the top, as it would suit when I had friends stay over. I woke up with extreme pain between my shoulder blades; it was so severe I could have cried. My best friend who was staying the night asked if I was OK. I was lying on my stomach and she saw that I had a spot of blood the size of a fist soaking my shirt. She panicked and screamed for my mom. When she came in and found

I had a wound which resembled a human bite mark she convinced herself that it was the cat.

I had to get it cleaned and bandaged by my friend's mom who is a nurse. She agreed it looked human and I told her I was in a fight and didn't want to tell my mom.

Then came the night that I thought the occurrences could not be ignored, my 14 yr old brother saw a person looking in his window which was nearly 7 foot off the ground. My Dad ran outside to look. The ground under Joey's window was soaked and muddy but not disturbed. My Mom and Dad was puzzled and once again stated, "You were having a nightmare". My brother wasn't convinced.

In March of the same year, my 12 year-old sister awoke from a nightmare. She climbed out of her bed and was intending to climb in beside me. But when she walked around the corner she saw a man bent over me and about an inch from my face. She screamed and he vanished. She then admitted to me she had seen lots of things in the house and had been too embarrassed to tell.

Finally it all ended as our landlord sold our house out from under us and we were forced to move; I was 21 years old and was sent to dorms to further my education.'

Certainly an experience like that is not one that should be taken lightly and is sure to be hard to forget.

Of course not all hauntings are meant to be harmful, but sometimes they can still scare the hell out of you even if they are not meant to. Take this next story given to us from DC.

An Unfamiliar Familiar Face

'About 5 years ago my husband, (boyfriend at the time), and I were renting an apartment in Waterville, Maine, USA. We'd gone to bed one evening and I was having a hard time falling asleep, tossing and turning in bed. At the time our bed room was set up in such a way that if you were laying in bed you could see out the bedroom door even though it was off to the left of the bed. Well in my tossing and turning I happened to roll over and see a man looking into the bedroom through the doorway. He was situated in such a way that he was peeking around the doorjamb so I could only see from his chin up. When he noticed me moving and looking at him he moved out of the doorway very quickly so I could no longer see him.

Well, I was paralysed with fear. I thought there was a man in our apartment either wanting to rob us or hurt us and was just waiting for me to go back to sleep so he could go through with his plan. I couldn't move, I was so scared I just lay there trying to figure out what I should do. Well it was only about 2 minutes later when I saw the man peek around the door again. This time, since I was so scared, I just laid there; I couldn't have moved if I'd wanted to. The man, satisfied we were sleeping I assume, proceeded to walk past the bedroom door and entered our bathroom. I didn't know what to do, I was so scared. This man was around 6 feet tall, probably 225 – 250 lbs and had short, dark hair. He was wearing a red flannel shirt with the sleeves torn off, jeans, and work boots. And now, he was stuck in my bathroom!

Now I'm really scared because once you were in the bathroom there was no place to go. He was going to have to turn around and come back by the bedroom to leave; there wasn't even a bathroom window for him to climb out. At this point I had to wake my boyfriend up. I gently shook Ray to wake him up but put my hand over his mouth and whispered "don't say anything" in his ear when I saw his eyes open. Well this freaked him out, but he didn't say a word. I moved my hand and whispered, "there's a man in our bathroom!" He looked at me with really big eyes and mouthed "WHAT?!" I just shook my head yes, I couldn't say it again. Well he quietly moved the covers, got up and grabbed his hunting knife from the floor of the closet and tiptoed to the bathroom. I remained frozen to the bed, just watching what I could see through the bedroom door.

He stepped out of the bedroom facing the bathroom and said "Who the hell do you think you are," in the sternest voice he could. I didn't hear a response. Then I could see Ray had turned the bathroom light on and I heard him open the shower curtain and shut the bathroom door and open it again. He came back into the bedroom and said, "What the hell is wrong with you, there is nobody in our bathroom."

I couldn't believe it. I told him what I'd seen and said, "You have to check the rest of the apartment. Maybe while I was waking you up he snuck back by the bedroom." Ray, annoyed but seeing how scared I was he knew I wasn't just screwing around, proceeded to check every closet and cupboard in our apartment. There was no man there. All the windows were locked just like when we went to bed, with all the screens still in them. The front door was still locked just like when we'd gone to bed. There was no one in our apartment but us. I never seen him again, but thinking about that night still gives me goose bumps.

Several months passed, Ray and I went to a Spiritualist Church with my family. We sat through the service and the medium seemed very gifted so I decided I was going to ask them if they could tell me who I'd seen in our apartment a while ago. After the service I approached the medium and asked, "Can you possible tell me who I might have seen in my apartment a couple months ago. It had to have been a spirit, but I didn't recognise the person." It only took a couple seconds and the medium said, "I'm being told his name was Hack and he wasn't there to scare or hurt you." That was all the medium could tell me. I said, "Okay, thank you. I don't know a 'Hack' but I'll ask around my family and see what I can learn." I told Ray what I had just learned and he just looked at me dumb founded and said, "What? What was the name?" A little confused by his response I said "Hack, do you know a Hack?" He said, "Yes, Hack was my grandfather's nickname and thinking back, he looked just like you described that night.'

It is true that sometimes in death, familiar faces will come back to check up on us, which is a nice thought but can be frightening just the same.

It is important to note that we as a people are not the only victims in a haunting, let's not forget or favoured pets, those creatures that can offer us so much loyalty and friendship yet can be just as frightened as us during those dark nights. This story is brought to us by DD.

Canine Perception

'I am 40 years old now and still do not have an understanding as to "why me"? I recall vividly beginning at the age of 5 being woken in the middle of the night by the noises of growls and the smell of something beyond belief. Having pillows yanked out from beneath my head and (pillows) being tossed across the room. Being so frightened that *breathing was not an option. Telling anyone about this was unheard of. This has happened to me countless times throughout my life. The only other being that has actually witnessed this would be my pets. They would growl or moan and react violently to these sounds that I thought only I could hear. The sound of someone scratching their nails on wood and low rumbling moans. To me this could mean only one thing, and I cannot bring myself to say it out loud.*

I am a Christian, I believe in God. There is no doubt about it. Which brings me back to this same question "why me"? Growing up literally learning to live (or sleep) through these noises have become almost a mundane part of life. On more than one occasion I have seen enormous black figures walk right in front of me almost taunting me in broad daylight. At the same time leaving a smell behind that would make the strongest of stomachs dry heave. My two Chihuahuas will bark uncontrollably at absolutely nothing that is visibly there on many occasions. At one point, the younger of my two dogs barked at my screen door that goes out to my patio and lunged at it as if someone was right there. Her hair stood on high end and she literally ran in circles. This is how she acts when there actually is someone visibly at my door.

Recently I was woken in the middle of the night at approximately 3 in the morning to the most excruciating pain in my left arm. I ran to the bathroom and turned on the light and found a bruise that I know for a fact was not there before. The first time this happened to me, I was so frightened that taking a photo of it was the farthest thing from my mind. It was a very large bruise that resembled a bite mark on my upper right arm. It was extremely black and sore as heck. And as quickly as I woke up from a sound sleep to find this bruise, it was amazingly gone. But a dark blotch still remains. This has affected me to the point that I now see a counsellor on a regular basis and I thank The Lord above that he does not find me absolutely insane. He is the only other person that I have told about these incidents until now.

I have two children, a son whom is 18 and my daughter who is 15. I know for a fact this has never happened to them, nor will I subject them to my horror by telling them about the things that have happened to myself. I say the "Guardian Angel Prayer" every night before bed in hopes this will end. But here I am, 35 years later and no end in sight to this unspeakable presence that has haunted me continuously. I did attempt to have the Deacon of my Church bless my home, his response was "If I believe a sinister presence is in my home, it will never leave, not even with a blessing." Is this true? Does having something like this happen to a person make them a believer of something evil and if so, does it mean that they aren't a Christian? NO! I will continue saying my prayers and living everyday for God.'

But there are times when we learn of happy endings to such happenings as sometimes things find a way of mending themselves if enough time is awarded to them.

Take for instance this story from JB.

The Secret Passage

'My first experience with the paranormal happened when my family moved to an old home in New Hampshire. The house was built in 1830 and moved off the side of a mountain in 1850 to the land it is currently standing upon.

We moved to this home in 1976 when I was 10 years old. One day, my mother had sent me down to the cellar to gather up the clothes we had hanging to dry. I never felt comfortable in that cellar. It was cold, dark and full of shadowy corners.

The old, rickety wooden stairs that shook and creaked when stepped upon, only added to the creepiness of that place. I always had the feeling of someone watching my every move while I was in the cellar, which caused me to never spend any more time down there than what was necessary. This one day, as I reached the bottom of the stairs with the laundry basket in hand, I looked to the left. What I saw startled me to the point of almost dropping the laundry basket. I saw a man standing there looking directly at me. His image is one I will carry with me my whole life. He wasn't a tall man, as I was about five foot, six inches at the time and had to stoop in the cellar. He was standing up straight and was as solid looking as anyone who is alive. He looked as though he was in his early forties, and a well-worn forties at that. He wore a wide, flat brimmed hat that covered his brown hair and had no facial hair except for his thick eyebrows that matched the colour of his hair. His clothes were that of a typical farmer from the previous century, white button down shirt, baggy trousers the colour of grey charcoal held up by suspenders, a brown overcoat that ended mid thigh and looked a bit big on him, dark boots that looked as though they had walked behind a plough for many years. His hands were thick and meaty, as you would expect of a man who laboured his whole life to earn a living for his family. I turned to my right to gather up the laundry as quickly as I could, cursing myself for dropping a few pieces of clothing in my hurried state. I dreaded turning around for fear I might see him still standing there watching me. When I turned to run up the stairs as fast as my fear would force me, much to my relief, he was no longer there. Every time since that day when I had to go down into the cellar, I refused to look to my left as I got to the bottom of the stairs. Even though I could still feel him watching me while I was down there, I didn't want to see him. The fear of seeing him again was too great for my young mind to handle.

A few years had passed and not much had happened as far as activity, save for the occasional *noise that was not a normal sound for a house. I eagerly dismissed those noises as being caused by one of my family members, or the cat. There was a pantry in the kitchen, which I was told to clean and organise by my mother to keep me busy on a day I had foolishly said I was bored. While I was cleaning the shelves, I noticed the bottom shelf was not as deep as the others, so I knelt down on the floor to look at it. It was then that I realised it wasn't a shelf at all, it was a step. It was the bottom step to a staircase that had been boarded up and made into a pantry. This hidden staircase was directly above the staircase that goes down to the cellar and lead to what we called the attic. It wasn't really an attic as the far as the true meaning of the word goes, just two unfinished rooms on the second floor of the house we used for storage. The attic was also another area of that house where I never felt comfortable and dared not spend much time in as it gave me the same feelings the cellar did. As luck would have it, after one of my sisters moved out, I was moved into the bedroom that shared a wall with the attic, and the door to the attic was in that bedroom. I would lay awake at night trying to sleep, but it was difficult. The head of my bed was against the wall that the attic shared and the door between the two rooms was on that wall, just to the right of my bed. I would hear things moving around in the attic late at night. I would try to convince myself it was just the mice that shared the house with us, but that was of no use. Mice didn't knock on the walls. Mice didn't make banging noises like the ones I heard. Mice didn't wear boots while walking across the floor. Nor were mice able to rattle the door handle. Sleep was something I didn't get much of during the time I lived in that room and I was very thankful when I moved into another room away from the attic.*

During my teen years, there were many times when I was alone in the house. I would be on the first floor and hear boots walking on the floor above me. Doors on the second floor would sometimes slam shut on their own. Yet, there were no windows or doors that were open to cause a draft big enough to slam a door shut. I took to listening to the television and radio rather loudly when I was home alone. It helped to convince my mind that what was going on wasn't actually happening. I was not the only person in the house to experience these things. My mother recently told me the same things would happen to her when she was home alone. Good, I thought, it wasn't just me and my overactive imagination.

About 10 years after I moved away from that house, my mother and one of my sisters decided to open the hidden staircase. Some say that restoration projects can stir up the paranormal. This was not the case here. Since that staircase was opened up, the activity stopped and has yet to return. I was very relieved to move away from that house and it took 14 years before I would return. I must admit, I was a bit apprehensive about stepping back into the home that frightened me as a young girl. However, my apprehension was put at ease the moment I crossed the threshold. I no longer felt the entities who resided there with us so long ago. The house had returned to the feeling of just an old farmhouse that has no more stories to tell.'

And that leaves us also with "no more stories to tell", so let's move into how you live with experiences such as these.

It is important to remember that a certain level of understanding is crucial in sharing space with the people of yesteryear. Make sure you know what you are dealing with. Is it a residual type of haunting that doesn't seem to take notice of you at all and just goes about its business? Is it an intelligent spirit who seems maybe just as confused as you are as to what is going on? Maybe they even want to know why you are in *their* space?

If the spirit does appear to be intelligent you should vocally make it known that this place is your place and that their time has passed. If you want them out, you should vocalise this, repeating that this is in fact your home and not theirs and that you wish them to leave. It may sound silly, and probably feel even more so as you stand there talking to someone who isn't there- but it is imperative that you lay down some basic ground rules and establish a general level of understanding of your wishes and the situation.

Sometimes it can be very easy to share your space with a spirit who means no harm. It has been noted in many reported cases of a haunting that activity remains at a minimum or at least peaceful if the homeowner or occupant talks respectfully to the spirit. This can be done by simply a general acknowledgment when you enter the room or arrive at home.

It is tantamount that if you should find you have intelligent and peaceful spirits in your home that you act respectfully as you would towards your own grandmother. Keeping in mind that these were once people like you and I; people who held jobs, had struggles, dreamed dreams, experienced heartbreak and love and all else that goes along with the human experience.

The stories you read are primarily from the USA but as the book continues we explore the world of the paranormal viewed by other cultures, faiths and beliefs. We would like to share a few of their stories, an insight into their homes, lives, and their hauntings. Although the world has gotten smaller due in part to global travel in pockets the world is as big as a universe and still full of as much mystery.

Live, love and play.

Chapter 3
Cultural views

"A house is never still in darkness to those who listen intently; there is a whispering in distant chambers, an unearthly hand presses the latch of the window, the latch rises. Ghosts were created when the first man awoke in the night."

J.M. Barrie

The following is designed to help those plagued with an unwanted haunting. Within the following pages we will share the viewpoints of many different people from different cultures, religious beliefs and spiritual views.

Please note that as the authors of this book, we have made every effort possible to interview as many individuals that we could in order to get a broad view that would be truly representative of each culture.

Due to the natural sociological fragmentation that has occurred over the centuries, many views have been adapted to reflect the changing of the times. It is also important to realise the modification that comes with the spreading out of families and thus the changes that occur within traditions. This is why some of the ways that are listed here may be different from those that you or someone you know may acknowledge or practice.

It has been our good fortune to be able to travel and meet with those who have been very willing to share their knowledge and allow this project to come together. Many cultures and faiths have brought us wonderful information and in some cases it was astonishing for us to see the similarities in some belief systems that will be explained as you read.

It is with great regret that we must report we have also unfortunately encountered some with a great reluctance to share their knowledge in some areas as it only further
inhibits all that we are trying to accomplish. However we do the best we can and press on in an effort to advance this field as much as we can, as much as those with the knowledge will allow it to go.

Dustin and Barry will not pass judgment on those unwillingly to share their insight, as it is far from their place or nature to do so, but it does reflect on the unfortunate hindrances in this field.

Tackling a subject so vast does have its challenges, one of which is simple organization. Do we divide it according to belief systems, practices or locations?
We decided the best way to present it was geographically.
In the following portion of the book you will see views presented according to the Continents in which they were gathered.

In this way you will explore the field as we did, through countless months of travel. Fortunately for you, you need not deal with customs and the questionable cuisine that has plagued us for so long. We remind you that these notes were derived and compiled from numerous interviews and do not necessarily always represent the views of the authors.

Of course the regular way of taking care of the situation on your own is the good old salt and water technique described by many in the west and is described in the following paragraphs below.

However the more common western approach to claiming back your home involves pure salt, preferably sea salt and water mixed together.

When mixing them it is best to use a prayer during this process such as 'May the blending of the elements of salt to preserve the sanctity and water cleanse this space, in the Name of ....' of course at this point due to all the mixed cultures in the west we will leave it up to the reader to add in their preferred religious icon. But you must concentrate on this with as much mind and physical power as possible. Speed is your worst enemy during this process, you must remain focused, determined and cover each corner, each dark area, each cupboard. When you do this you must mean it and most of all you must feel it.

Take the water and with your fingers lightly sprinkle the blessed water around every room every door and every window and paying particular attention to entry points into your home. It's almost like a spiritual spring clean for your home which should be done once a month.

Our own comprehension of this reality is reflected in the understanding of many parents when we speak about keeping our homes clean. This is also true for the life of your home spiritually, as a filthy home will attract flies.

Some followers of this technique would suggest lighting white candles in each room with some sweet incense containing an element of sage, whilst others would insist on placing a bunch of fresh flowers into the main room of the house, however in the older belief systems this was used to feed the pranic energy, the energy every living creature produces and needs to live and this would supply some support for those recently deceased whilst the soul broke free from the body.

But what about other people around the world, what processes do they use and why?

ASIA

Brief history of Asia and Culture

Early settlers to Asia predominantly were found around the coast and these early people went on to evolve as a society and build and develop, leading to the development of some of the planets earliest known civilisations. In order to give the reader an idea of the extent of their work and development recent archaeological digs has found evidence of stone tools in Malaysia dating to approximately 1.83 million years old.

However it was in western Asia that we finally saw the world's earliest transition to settled farming with the development of crops and the keeping of livestock lighting the way for the evolution from hunter to farmer.

Many thousands of years later and countless wars the influence of the silk road played an immeasurable part on the development of many ancient civilisations which connected China, India, the Middle East and of course Europe. As wealth and food stores increased incredibly, natural migration of cultures occurred spreading religions throughout Asia such as Hinduism and Buddhism, which became a great influence on South, East and Southeast Asia.

The Asian Experience

Our first stop in this paranormal journey of learning is the mighty continent of Asia.

Spirit and ancestry are very important throughout the Asian continent and islands. The big hitters such as China, Japan, Indonesia, and of course Malaysia have a diverse approach to haunting's and sometimes they even take measures to ensure such an occurrence will not happen.

A good example of such precaution is the Petronas Twin Towers in Kuala Lumpur, Malaysia. They are reported to be the fifth highest buildings in the world, even catching recent attention during our visit there as the French free-climber Alain Robert, who scaled to the top of one of the towers without any harness or safety equipment, and was subsequently arrested for his accomplishment. It was indeed quiet the remarkable feat of endurance and may have even caught the attention of the spirits in the building as he climbed by their windows, for you see, within the towers themselves, spirits are held very sacred.

According to the locals, after construction was completed in 1998 a local spiritual consultant was contacted in order to address the spirits within the building. On behalf of the building owners he negotiated a deal with the spirits that one floor would remain free of any offices and would be completely set aside for the spirit world. No trouble within the building has since been reported and all seems quite peaceful. But of course this is looking at prevention and bolting the stable door before the horse has ran off, which in itself is a reversal of the metaphor and is something practiced rarely in the financial institutions in western culture these days.

With the stage set and the importance of the spirit world in Malaysia well noted, we enter into our first interview that is rather intriguing.

The Spirit World as Explained by a Malaysian Muslim

In Malaysia we had the unique opportunity to speak with a local "Cure Man" who works within the community dealing with spirits that plague those of the Muslim faith.

As a Cure Man it is his responsibility to work with those who feel that their home is haunted, or if they have been possessed by a demon or have trouble with one of the Jinn.

He tells us that those in the Muslim faith do not believe in ghosts at all. The human spirit passes on after this life and does not stay here. What dwells with us here on Earth are demons and the Jinn.

The Jinn appear in both Islamic and pre Islamic texts and are seen as an entity that has the ability of free will. It is believed Iblis was the first Jinn or Genie not to bow to the control of Adam as instructed by God according to the Islamic holy text, the Qur'an.

The original word *Jinn* in Arabic simply means *hidden* and in this case refers to the Jinn as being a form which is unseen, remaining invisible, or by its very term hidden. The Jinn are from the smokeless fire and the Earth; they have always been here, before even Adam and Eve. They made a promise to God that they would, at any cost, do whatever it takes to endlessly test our faith, to test our loyalty to and our trust within the one true God.

There are two types of Jinn, one good and one bad. The good Jinn can be very helpful in protecting families and leading them to a better life. The bad Jinn can be very destructive, ruining lives and tearing apart families.

The Jinn exist in a different dimension than we do, but at times these dimensions come very close. Sometimes we hear of someone whom has crossed over into the realm of the Jinn. Though they may feel as if they were only gone a mere matter of minutes, it may have been months or years in our time. (*Note: We also see this concept within the Irish concept of the Fairy legends*)

The difference between Jinn and demons is this: A demon cannot physically harm a human on its own; it can only influence the way a person thinks and acts. Demons need to possess a body, a human, before they can physically act out in such a way to harm another human being.

The Jinn do not need to do this. The Jinn do not possess people and are quite capable of both physically harming and influencing human beings.

The Jinn become involved with people of the Muslim faith because people make deals with them. Some of the common deals he has come across have been made for the protection of the family and for their well-being, be it financially or whatever the person desires. But, the Jinn must be paid. Often a person will offer their children to the Jinn, this is what he believes happens in the cases of phantom births, where a woman appears pregnant for a time and then the baby is suddenly taken from the womb without any sign of miscarriage. He believes in this instance that the Jinn take the child as payment for the deal.

As a Cure Man, if someone approaches him for help, his first priority is to determine what the damages are and whom they were done by, either Jinn or demon. As he said, it is easy to determine, as he only needs to see if the person is possessed to know that he is dealing with a demon since the Jinn cannot possess a human.

It is the job of a Cure Man to expel these demons from their host bodies through a series of prayers from the Koran and blessings with Holy Water throughout the home and upon the person. Only through
the Koran can this be accomplished within the Muslim faith. Once a demon has
been banished, the person will be forever cleared of that demon.

If it is Jinn that he is dealing with, he must talk with the family members to find out if a deal was made with the Jinn and what that deal was. What was the purpose and what was the payment.

It is possible that sometimes an elder member of the family had made a deal with the Jinn but passed away before they could release the Jinn of their duties. In such cases the Jinn passes to the eldest member of the family. If for some reason that family member rejects the Jinn, then trouble can start and the Jinn may decide to cause harm to that person or unto that family.

Elder members of the family should release the Jinn of their agreement before they die, but, since we don't not know the time at which we will die, this can cause a problem.

This is where the Cure Man comes in and fulfills a crucial role to returning the family to peace and freeing the Jinn, or, if need be, killing the Jinn.

The Cure Man will talk with the Jinn and find out what it wants. Most times the negotiation is very easy and they may demand something as simple as the preparation of a special meal and the construction of a small boat. The food is placed upon the boat and sailed down river or into the sea. Negotiations will vary based on the different types of Jinn.

If the Jinn will not deal, then it is up to the Cure Man to decide if the Jinn must be killed.
It is important to remember that the Jinn are also God's creatures and that they are loyal to God, and sometimes they are here to teach us lessons, if the Cure Man makes the wrong decision, he will hear it from the remaining Jinn.

Only the intervention of a Cure Man can resolve a problem with the Jinn, be it the fulfillment of the deal, a negotiation, or the death of the Jinn. Unlike with demons, the clearing of a person, a family or a home of the Jinn is not necessarily permanent. The Jinn could return if they are asked to by another human whom has made a deal with the Jinn to do so. As you can see, dealing with the Jinn can be very tricky.

It is important in life to remember that the Jinn are always active within our lives, but even more so when they are provoked, so people should use caution and show respect.

Respect is key in living your life with the Jinn. If you do not show them respect they can tear apart your life, harming you and the ones you love. All people should also be respected, throughout all religions, as it is his belief that all are connected.

A Japanese Buddhist

A few hours across the China Sea will bring you to Japan, a land that surprised us greatly and we can only hold but the greatest respect for this island nation of technology and farming. We have never come across such a class of people with such polite mannerisms.

And as in all other aspects in which we experienced, when it came to sharing their views and understandings of the spirit world, they could not have been more helpful.
Of course the main religion in Japan is Buddhism and it is very apparent. Even as we were handed our tickets by the airline staff they reached out to us as if it was a gift to us in their open hands and bowed their heads as we accepted.

Buddhism is a religion first taught by Siddhartha Gautama more commonly known as Buddha or the awakened one.

He taught near where he was born in Nepal and never ventured much further than the northeastern region of the Indian sub-continent until his death around 400 BC. It took some time for the religion to spread but by the 2nd century BC it had reached Asia and today it one of the big hitters in the religious field with estimates of 500 million followers worldwide.

The houses of worship in Japan are regarded very highly and are of incredible importance. It is believed the Vajrapani guard the temples; a deity thought to protect not only the temples worldwide, but also the Buddha himself.

We spoke with a Buddhist woman from Japan who had practiced the Buddhist faith along with Japanese customs since her childhood. English was not her native tongue of course, but she did very well in communicating to us what needed to be said. Our very question of the importance of the spirit world caused her to giggle, as if to say, of course the spirit world is important to my culture.

She is also married to a Buddhist Reverend and thus is very intimately acquainted with the ways of the faith as it was taught in Japan. She spoke of the extreme importance of the spirit world as it relates to ours and how the Obake (spirits) are very respected by the Japanese people. This is the reason they have the Obon festival every year.

Image of Vajrapani captured at the Buddhist Temple in Singapore. Photo by Barry Fitzgerald 2008.

That is why they have the Obon festival every year in Japan which is usually celebrated on July 15 in accordance with the Lunar calendar or August 15 if timed with the Solar calendar. The Obon, or just Bon, is also referred to as "Day of the Dead," and it is a Japanese Buddhist custom designed to honour the departed spirits of one's ancestors. This custom has evolved into a magnificent family reunion during which people return to ancestral family places to visit and clean their ancestors' graves, paying their respects to those who came before them. This time is also said to be the opportunity for spirits of ancestors to revisit the household altars they may have worshiped at during life.

The Obon is also referred to as the Feast of Lanterns and has been celebrated in Japan for more than 500 years. These festivities usually include a dance around a high tower in the middle of the dance ring known as Bon-Odori and a ceremonial drum known as the Taiko is played loudly, so that the angels and the spirits of loved ones, can hear it and know they are not forgotten.

Interestingly enough, it was during this very festival that we were able to gather this information from this woman whom was gracious enough to share her information with us.

There is more to the celebration than meets the eye, for it is believed that on these days it is the only time the iron pot in hell is opened for the deceased. In Japan they light paper lanterns and are then floated down rivers symbolically signaling the ancestral spirits' return to the world of the dead.

Private Buddhist services are held all over Japan in homes of families whilst friends are invited over to share food and honour those who have passed, especially those whom had passed within the year. The significance of sharing food dates back to the story of Mokuren, a disciple of Buddha, who used his supernatural powers to look upon his deceased mother. He saw that she had fallen into the Realm of Hungry Ghosts and was suffering. The student was terribly upset and so he went to Buddha and asked how he could release his mother from this realm. Buddha instructed him to make offerings to the many Buddhist monks who had just completed their summer retreat, on the fifteenth day of the seventh month. Upon completion of this task the disciple finally saw his mother released from the clutches of that realm.

He also began to see and to understand the true nature of her past unselfishness and the many sacrifices that she had made so that his life would be that much better. The student became so overwhelmed with joy for his mother's release and grateful for his mother's kindness and thus danced with joy.

It was in this act that signified the beginning of the Bon Odori, a time in which ancestors and their sacrifices are remembered and appreciated.

Of course there are variations to the Bon Dance due in part to geographical differences, but we were told that traditionally the Japanese are only ones who dance in the ring.

The Obon festival is a tell tale sign of how important the spirit world is and how much reverence is given to those who came before us. (Note: This whole concept of dancing in rings and communing with spirit is certainly not a new thing it has been around for thousands of years. Ancient man used circles to commune with spirit guides, ancestors and even their gods, right back into ancient Greece it was seen as a way to talk to their gods.)

In terms of how a home can become haunted, she tells us that she believes it happens when a spirit has unfinished business here on Earth. She says a haunting can also occur if there is a personal object that the spirit loved in their lifetime that is now in someone else's possession. She also notes that a spirit may linger in a location where a life has been lost, or near the final resting place of the body.

In terms of dealing with a haunting she stated that these are the types of things her husband deals with and that it is customary to have a Buddhist Priest conduct a prayer service within the home, along with all of the occupants of the house present, in an attempt to guide the wrestles soul to peace.

This cleansing process requires ceremonial robes, the chanting of Japanese Psalms as well as the burning of copious amounts of incense.

Incense sticks are lit using the continuous light of the previous family member's incense, then all of the incense is placed within a ceremonial bowl, the ashes are prayed over, pinched within the fingers, held to the forehead of those who live within the dwelling. A metal incense burner suspended from chains is used by the Priest as he spreads the incense throughout the home and completes the blessing. Then a meal is served, prayed over, and shared amongst the family and the Priest.

In Japan the art of Blessing is a ceremony that is seen to bring positive energy into the home and business. Both business and the home are a very important aspect in the lives of the Japanese and can relate to increased security and well-being and is often treated like a living object as it needs to be taken care of and loved to sustain the harmony of the home life.

The blessings seen as a form of substance that aims to "feed" the house and show proper treatment and respect to it in order to create a sense of peace, balance and harmony. The home is seen and recognized as being important to family life and actually becomes part of the family in its own way.

This ceremonial process is often effective in calming or removing a disruptive spirit. However it is not entirely uncommon for the spirit to return, or another one to come forth in its place, at which time you must invite the Buddhist Priest's to come once again and perform a follow up ceremony.

She says this is why the Obon is so important. Its purpose is to send the restless souls away from the living while also honouring those who have passed so that they will remain rested knowing they are remembered, comforted by not being forgotten. Once again we see how respect and honour for the dead, reverence for the spirits, is held with such high regard.

The Shinto Belief in Japan

Staying in Japan for just a few more moments, we would be remiss not to mention the belief system known as Shinto. It incorporates spiritual practices derived from many local traditions, but did not emerge as a formal centralised religious institution until the arrival of Confucianism, Daoism, and Buddhism. Kami-no-michi is the natural spirituality of Japan and the Japanese people, very similar to Paganism within the Celtic lands of Europe. The word Shinto means "Way of the Gods" and this belief system reflects that in how it perceives the connection that we all possess within the sacredness found in nature.

Shinto is a religion in where ritual and practice, rather than mere words, are of the utmost importance. Known for its worship of nature, ancestors, polytheism, and animism, with a strong focus on ritual purity, involving honouring and celebrating the existence of Kami.

In English Kami would be defined as "spirit" or "deities"; some cases being animistic, others more like mankind, and then there are those associated with more abstract "natural" forces in the world.

It also recognises the presence of deities in trees, rivers, thunderstorms, waterfalls, mountains, rocks, and valleys. The elements and their energies are thought of and regarded as sacred. These 'Kami' are worshiped as gods, as well as, the ancestral and guardian spirits, but the spirits of national heroes also get thrown into the mix. The Sun Goddess, Amaterasu is the leader of the Kami, and is thought to be the patron deity of Japan.

The followers of Shinto use things like Talismans and Amulets for their personal protection ensuring good fortune. Made of paper, wood, or metal, the Ofuda talisman has to be given to you by a Shinto priest at one of their many shrines, it is inscribed with the name of a Kami and is used for protection within one's home.

It's intriguing that they practice the Kagura, an ancient Shinto ritual dance in which music is played in such a way as to encourage the Kami to dance with the people and something similar is seen in Voodoo ceremonies. These songs are performed to summon the gods as well as to ask for blessings and answers to prayers.

There are also ceremonies performed at funerals in order to appease the spirits of the departed so that may rest. Once again we see the importance of remembering those who have passed on before us and the respect that is still held for departed ancestors.

The followers of Shinto assume that the Kami are the only things that have a great and direct influence on their daily lives but distinguish that they are neither good nor bad and they also understand that everything is sacred with no separation between the material and spiritual world.

The Kami spirits and the people are never thought of as separate for they exist within the same world which is an important thing to keep in mind as we all grow together, not just with each other, but also with the Earth itself.

With that we now leave Asia and head off to North America, a melting pot of belief systems if there ever was one

Americas

A brief history lesson

South America is speculated to have been first inhabited by people crossing the Bering Land Bridge from Asia, more commonly known as the Bering Strait. It has been proposed that this same land bridge was used by the Gigantis Gigantopithecus, a huge ape which stood some 8 feet tall when on his back legs and has been suggested maybe the origin behind the legends of the Yeti allegedly found in the Himalayas, north of India.

The earliest permanent settlement discovered in South America dates from 3500 BC located by the Valdivia on the coast of Ecuador but the highly successful Caral Supe civilisation were noted as one of the oldest civilisations in the Americas and strangely enough have shown absolutely no sign of warfare a very unusual thing to happen considering the region. Before the arrival of the Europeans it was estimated there were some 30 million people living in South America.

When the Europeans appeared throughout the Americas it seems they were very generous with gifts such as smallpox, influenza, measles and typhus which were passed onto the native cultures severely crippled their numbers and in many cases destroyed whole tribes. With the passing of several hundred years growing dissatisfaction with British rule,...I know, I know it's hard to believe, but the thirteen British colonies in north America issued a

Declaration of Independence in 1776 and successfully fought the British army and became known as the Revolutionary War or the War of Independence. Of course the British still never got over the destruction of so much tea in the Boston harbour, I can only imagine the Royal family would have needed revived with smelling salts when told.

One hundred and fifty years later and following WW2 north America, or rather the United States of America since the War of Independence became a world superpower sparking the Cold War with the Soviet Union. The cool heads of Ronald Reagan (1911 – 2004) the former President then of the USA and Premier Meikhail Gorbachev (1931 – present) of the USSR brought about a thaw in the cold war. However with the collapse of the Soviet Union a few years later, the United States became the world's only superpower but was soon to be challenged by China.

The United States Of America

By its very history of immigration from across various seas, there are many concepts of religion and the spirit world within this land. Along with immigrants, foods, soil samples and disease, came many gods from all parts of the world. Our first stop in North America is, fittingly enough, with a representative of the Native American culture.

A Navajo & Apache Perspective

We were fortunate enough to have found someone who could speak to us from a most interesting and spiritual viewpoint, that of the native people of America, known as the Dine', the Southwest United States Native American tribe, and commonly as the Navajo and Apache people.

Our contact tells us that for all his life he has practiced Dine' spirituality in addition to a little of forced Catholicism. He says that the spirit world is a big part of his daily life. To better understand his daily life you have to understand the concepts of this world and the next a bit more. He lives on what he refers to as "Indian Time", with is to say "in the now". Yet here on Indian Time is where he receives messages from spirit guides, from those who have passed on, and, interestingly from those spirits who have never been "people".

The communication comes to him through various means, such as visions, dreams, voices, drumming, and sounds, though the messages are not restricted to solely these types of transport mediums. He says that he is still learning new things all the time and finding new ways by which the spirit world communicates with him.

It is important to note that there exists a measurable fear of repeating these types of things to the mainstream. He says that he has noticed this quite often when working with children from the Native-American culture. The children are hesitant to report their abilities for fear of being labeled "insane".

However within the Dine' belief system people with these abilities are not treated as "insane" at all for the Dine' highly regard the spirit world and treat spirits with the utmost respect. Even "Holy" people never assume that they have full understanding of what they are dealing with when dealing with the spirit world. All people therefore treat the spirits with due reverence and take nothing for granted.

In terms to a location becoming haunted, our interviewee shares with us a view that we find particularly intriguing. He says that within his belief system, the spirit worlds and our world come very close to each other as night falls. This is why most things tend to happen during the night time hours. The worlds being closer together greater enables and facilitates activity and interaction to occur.

He says that he lets spirits in all the time when asking for guidance in this world, but warns that others may come in as well. Not all of them bad though, he says he had a friend who has passed on, who "messes with" him from the next world as much as he did in this world.

Though there are spirits that he describes as "dark" or "black". These spirits tend not to be the most positive energies and there are many ways that they can enter our world and a lot of it has to do with balance.

In Dine' beliefs it is taught that everything has positive as well as negative energy within it. If there is too much positive or too much negative, then something is not right, something is not in balance. This can occur if someone is involved in some sort of tragedy, or they are going through a tough time and their energy is not well. An imbalance within or around oneself can be dangerous, as the darker spirits will usually enter where there is too much negative energy. This imbalance favouring the negative energies is what can cause darker spirits to come forth and to haunt a location or person. There exist other ways for these spirits to cross over as well, some people have also taken it upon themselves to call forward these darker spirits in order to do another harm or to spread ill will.

If a spirit becomes troublesome you can cleanse the negative energy by burning Sage and Sweetgrass while saying the right prayers and walking through every part of your house.

However, some tribes believe that in doing this you are getting rid of *all* spirits, so it is suggested that you are careful with doing this.

Medicine Men have suggested the burning or discarding of the personal belongings of those who have passed on; this is done in accordance to the belief that it will free the spirits of their attachment to the objects and to the space. If this fails to calm the spirit activity then the Medicine Men are brought in to perform rituals that those who are not Medicine Men are not privy to.

After these ceremonies and practices are conducted in hopes of alleviating the spirit activity the holy men will give families things to burn and prayers to say, so that whatever is troubling them will not return.

It is important to remember that if these spirits are coming forth in an attempt to simply get our attention, it's usually not to scare us but to give us messages and guidance, this is why it is not good to clear your home of all types of spirit and why the act of ritualistic cleansing is not one that is done simply upon a whim. It is important to respect the spirit world and to hear what they have to tell us.

The Southern Accent on the Afterlife

South of the Mason Dixon line we were able to interview a gentleman who was raised a Catholic and then spent some time exploring other faiths before becoming an ordained Southern Baptist minister. He offered us insight based on his own understandings of the paranormal and also shared with us how as a minister he handles situations should they arise.

Personally the spirit world is very important to him, but he also views himself as a little different than the average Christian person. He believes he is a little more open minded than some and probably more close-minded than others. Ultimately he has the highest regard for the spirit world because God is a spirit and he communicates with us through the Holy Spirit.

In regards to the spirit world and the people of his congregation, he says that there is a greater emphasis on certain parts of the understanding of the afterlife in regards to the Holy Spirit, which he believes to be the spirit of the living God. Some within the church believe in other spirits, however for the most part, the beliefs are that a spirit is good or evil, the influence of God or Satan.

As he mentioned, the spirit world is divided, the negative spirits being viewed as demonic and the positive ones as angelic. True demonic spirits never have been, nor ever
will be, human and the same goes for angels; there are specific scriptural references that speak to this.

He states that this division is just a general reference point; he personally feels that all spirits may not be that simple to interpret. In regards to human spirits in the afterlife, he believes that some of the personality traits the person demonstrated in life will no doubt carry over into death. Thus there are human spirits whom are not entirely good or evil, but a mix of that angelic/demonic influence that they would have reflected in their life on Earth.

He is reluctant to fully commit to the concepts of places being haunted. When presented with a situation of someone who feels as if they are dealing with a spirit he takes each case differently according to the impression he gets based upon the reports given to him.

Depending on what the people wish him to do about the situation also affects his approach to the problem. Not every spirit needs to be made to leave or persuaded to move on. There have been some exceptions that he has encountered, and at those times a combination of Holy Water, Anointing Oil and prayer does what needs to be done.

He tells us that he makes a point to try to help people understand how to clearly take authority of their own homes. This usually works as well, but of course some are quicker to grasp this concept than others and some need to be taken by the hand

and shown how to do this through various techniques of self-empowerment and faith.

Over the years he has had to help more people who felt like they were being personally haunted versus houses with spirit activity. He feels that if you are able to clear the person of their problems the problems within the home will sort themselves out.

However, in the case of a demonic entity within the home it is a different story. He usually asks the homeowner to leave the property for a period of time; usually an hour or so, though in some cases he has had the homeowner stay with him there while he uses the Holy Water, Anointing Oil and prayer to force the demon out.

He cautions that in his experience no two cases have been alike. Always relying on the clues provided to him and mixing in a little gut instinct has been the best recipe for handling the problems that have been brought before him. He also makes a point to ensure that there is a support system in place for those whom ask for his help so as not to leave them empty handed when his part of the job is done, though he is always available should they need his continued assistance.

We find it interesting in regards to his comments about the human spirit and the influence placed upon it in life, and thus carrying over into death. At what point will we be free of this spirit world tug of war?

The American Catholic

Back in the States, we were granted an insight from not only a Christian, but an ordained priest of the Roman Catholic Faith who has been involved with the faith all of his life.
He speaks to the importance of the spirit world in the Catholic faith, not just in terms of the human spirit, but also to a professed belief in angelic and demonic spirits, and most importantly, to the acknowledgment of the immortality of the soul after death.

He tells us that beyond mere beliefs, the Catholic faith also allows for certain types of accepted mystical experiences; from that of St. Michael in Italy, to Our Lady, (Mary the mother appearing) in so many places around the world from the early days of the Church to the present. Noted accounts are recognized in Portugal, France, Ireland, Mexico and Croatia to name a few. There are also accounts of human souls (mostly from Purgatory) appearing to chosen people.

As researchers, we find it intriguing to see the account of souls from Purgatory being mentioned. This has been a long held suspicion of many whom are active in their faith, yet question the existence of spirit activity within our own Earthly realm after we depart from our bodies.

Father also speaks to us about what we would classify as Inhuman entities. He reports on a created species called *Angels* that are good and many times serve as messengers from God as well as Heavenly Protectors. Some of these angels rebelled with Lucifer and fell, becoming forever demons or devils. These are evil that seek the ruin of souls and lead them away from God. This pagan myth of fallen angels was adapted by the early Christians and as the story developed and parts were added Lucifer translated from Hebrew to Latin means (Morning Star) but was replaced by Satan. This maybe a mistake as some theologians such as Father Jose Fortea and Father Amorth believe that Lucifer and Satan are very different beings. In the New Testament Lucifer disappears and is replaced by Satan as we can see in the books of the Gospels. In Islam the reference to Lucifer is known as Iblis, more commonly known as Shayṭān and we can see with a few word plays and Chinese whispers where in English we arrive at Satan. Iblis was made from the smokeless fire as with other Djinn but he was seen as proud and arrogant and would not bow to Adam as instructed by God. Hmmmm doesn't this ring a bell. However it still is a very shadowy area as Lucifer in Latin also refers to 'Light Bringer' and refers to the planet Venus in the early morning sky.

The concept of Satan as a great horned beast can be more linked with the god *Pan* and dates back to the days when Catholicism was battling it out with Paganism, a common practice back then to demonize the former faith in support of your own such as Beelzebub the Philistine god who also become thrown into the Christian mixing pot of names referring to the ultimate evil.

In some Christian followings Satan is in fact, one of the most beautiful, if not *the* most beautiful and cunning creation God has ever made. Hence the attraction to follow his ways and forever darken your soul. But enough about Satan, he needs no extra publicity, back to the interview.

Father mentions those human souls whom have crossed over and are part of the Heavenly Realm; these whom we call *Saints* who minister to us also and intercede on our behalf.

There are also good spirits whom are on the journey to God, and conversely there are damned souls who work in league with demons. Forever in an eternal battle for the possession of human souls; temptation versus redemption, and the cycle goes on.

He mentions that he also believes in crossed over souls who seek to watch over the living. We cannot help but wonder if this is a possible explanation for so many of the spirits of departed loved ones whom are witnessed countless times by grieving family members. It is also important to remember the role of and the recognition of the Holy Spirit and its position within the Trinity of God the Father and the Son.

Father has done a splendid job in outlining some of the hierarchy with the plains of Heaven and Hell, but what about our realm and how it comes to pass that these spirits intermingle with the living?

He says that houses can be haunted for several reasons:
- a human spirit is allowed to be here because the place was special to them.
- a human spirit is looking for some kind of resolve.
- a human spirit is attached to a particular person whom it is watching over or protecting.
- an evil spirit who wants dominance over a particular place or person.

These ideas seem to fit nicely with many investigators have been theorizing for some time and thus brings us to the next question, what can be done about it?

Father shares that if the house or property were believed to be experiencing paranormal activity, he would first suggest an experienced paranormal team and a reputable psychic be called in to investigate. Once the reason for the haunting is established, a decision should be made for the best resolve. If there were demonic presences there, the group should call in clergy or a seasoned and reputable "Warrior Group" to cleanse the house.

However, he is quick to point out that the prayers and traditional cleansings are not enough on their own. He says that the maintenance following the process is as important as the process itself. If it is a (human) spirit, then the resolve is an agreement between the clients and the spirit including boundaries. If the spirit has not yet crossed...someone should be called in to cross them over.

If there was deliverance or cleansing from evil spirits, a measure must be made to make sure the spirit does not return. This could mean removing clutter, making the house brighter and more positive. Regular use of holy water and religious images in the home as well as the mending of any strained relationships in the house should also take place. There may also be necessary lifestyle changes and the return to the practice of their Faith and daily prayers.

We concur that the follow up process is very important indeed. As with any faith, it is dependent upon the strength of the belief and the maintenance of said belief.

A Medicine Man and Medium from the Lakota Tribe

Within America exists many Native people whom have the utmost respect for the spirit world and those around us. We were fortunate to have spoken with a member of the Lakota. The Lakota were originally referred to as the Dakota when they lived by the Great lakes, however, because of European American settlement they were pushed away from the great lakes region and later called themselves the Lakota which became part of the Sioux.

The gentleman we spoke with is not only a member of the Lakota, but is also a gifted medium and Medicine Man. He was trained on the Pine Ridge Reservation in the tradition of Yuwipi, from the descendants of Crazy Horse. Though he is proud of his heritage and his status, he remarks that his abilities are not something that he boasts about.

He shares with us a bit of the Lakota way of life; he talks of The Great Spirit that he calls *Wakan Tanka*. From our research and understanding, Wakan Tanka is typically understood as the power or the sacredness that resides in everything. Wakan Tanka was to have placed the stones and minerals in the ground, change the seasons and weather, and make the plants come out of the ground.

He tells us that he believes in the sixteen expressions, or beings, of The Great Spirit Which are called *TOB TOB*, which loosely interpreted means "four times four".

Everything is based upon the original Concept of Directionology; the four directions, four beings, four races, four elements and the four sacred colors representing the race of Man. The number four itself is sacred among the Lakota. Spiritual Practice is cyclical following the seasonal changes.

He has practiced these ways and beliefs all of his life. He notes that Lakota Spirituality is not based upon Dogma but rather a way to live and act. The Lakota call this "Walking your talk". This belief is applied to what everyone's *Hanblechiyapi* or life vision is. One must always aspire to do their very best and they believe religion is the expression of this base fundamental concept. If you are Christian, Buddhist, Muslim, and so on, this is the individual soul's choice to express their fundamental right to believe as they would. He states that they do not have disagreements over religious dogma but rather they consider how The Great Spirit speaks to you is unique to the person's individual relationship with God.

As researchers it is key to realize how this understanding helps to speak to the commonality within the fundamental message of the major religions of the world.

Our Native medium says that the Spirit world is found in every fundamental aspect of life, for we are just passing through this temporary existence and thus we must acknowledge that which is eternal.

Spirits are first and foremost regarded with respect; as in most religions, the Lacota believe there are both benevolent and malevolent Spirits. The Lacota recognize spirits called Iktomi and Mayasleca (tricksters and poltergeist) as well as the *Chi Chi* (ghosts) and *Wanagi Spirits* (angels).

Spiritual harmony is something to be strived for. The Lakota believe that positive and negative are subjective; what is good for you may be bad for me and vice versa. They believe that true harmony can only be achieved when they are neutral. This is very evident during the packing of the Sacred *Canumpa* (pipe). During which they pray "Great Spirit I place before you all that is good and evil, for there is only one power at this, you Great Spirit".

They further believe that it the intention of a person's heart, *Washte Chante* "Good Heart" *Pejuta Washte* Good Medicine", that makes something truly good or truly evil.

In terms of why a home can become haunted and why a spirit would linger, they believe Chi-Chi or Iktomi can be attracted to us for various reasons; whether it is a deed we have done or something sent to us by one who practices evil or a skin-walker. (Skin-walkers are known in various cultures, often called shape shifters. To Native Americans skin-walker was one who could shift their appearance, often to that of an animal.)

Our friend from the Lakota says that Spirits linger because of unfinished business or due to an energetic attachment to the original place of a traumatic passing. The severity of this passing determines the severity of the haunting. He has assisted in various cases over the years. He was trained to discern not only the presence of Spirit, but also to observe their intention. All Lakota ceremony is focused around the understanding that everything is spiritually possessed, whether good or bad.

In order to assist those who are troubled by spirit activity, several things must take place. Communication to spirits is never done directly; they do no talk to the so-called dead. Those in Medicine roles study to develop a strong relationship with what they call a *Kola*, a spiritual guide friend believed to be sent directly to them by God to assist in our life's purpose. This Kola is then used as a buffer between them and the Spirit world and carries spiritual requests to The Great Spirit.

Instruction on how to deal with particular issues comes to them via a ceremony in direct communication to The Great Spirits will. However, even with this ceremony, information and details are given to them by way of the Kola.

To ward against hauntings and to disperse ghosts or tricksters, they use a special herb smudge called Wacaga (sweet grass) that travels between the seen and unseen worlds. Though they study many, many years to achieve this relationship with a Kola or Spiritual Guardian, it is a rarity to achieve this Connection.

Lastly, he reports that due to the commitment a Medicine Man makes to The Great Spirit, and the Carrying of The Sacred Canumpa, he can honestly say that he has never experienced a haunting of any situation he has been called in to handle.

Though we have spanned the globe and spoken with many whom have represented various viewpoints, this one speaks the most to Dustin as he is part Native American (Cherokee) and has long been interested in the connection made by the native people of North America with the spirit world. Particularly with the concept of the religious dogma understanding, and the intention of the human heart in its sway over what is good and evil.

The Lakota perspective once again shows the proper respect for the spirit world and the careful reverence with which it is approached, not to mention a success rate of 100% when carried out by a properly trained Medicine Man; however we are reminded how difficult and rare the connection of such a level is to come by.

A Hawaiian Catholic Recipe

Next up we look to the Pacific Island of Hawaii, which falls under the umbrella of North America by being part of the United States.

A native from the isle of O'ahu was kind enough to share a unique viewpoint of an islander raised according to Catholicism.

Within her heritage of Hawaiian and Chinese (to name a few), the spirit world has been impressed upon her as being very important and an integral part of this life. She believes strongly in the power of God and in accessing that power through prayer and the saying of the rosary.

She says that spirits are very much here with us, all around us, and that, if need be, they will make themselves known. Therefore she always asks before picking up certain items and she says "please" and "thank you" for things throughout her day-to-day life; a constant sign of respect is shown to those spirits whom are present, yet remain unseen. She starts each and every day by welcoming the elements in the morning by simple verbal communication, greeting them as she would any person that you would meet. Candles and stones are used for luck, guidance and solace.

In order to be forewarned of entities that may be approaching her she often watches her dreams, as guiding spirits will sometimes warn her there.

The interaction with and acknowledgment of the spirit world is extremely important to her belief system and "nothing to laugh at". The spirits are held in such very high regard that she has made it of great importance to teach her children to understand and to respect the spirit world as well.
In regards to how a location can become haunted, it is her belief that this can occur if something tragic and truly awful occurred to a person quite suddenly. Perhaps they were in such a good place in their life at the time that they don't really realize that they are gone. She likens it to childhood memories that remind you of happier times; perhaps to a spirit, not being alive is incredibly devastating and so they remain here, clinging desperately to a happy and familiar place.

When troublesome or evil spirits are encountered she simply opens the front and back door of her dwelling, vocally commands the spirits to leave and informs them that they do not belong here with her. She says she can usually feel the cold whoosh of them passing by as they are leaving.

Her next step involves the sprinkling of Holy Water around the house and then she also dabs a bit onto each child. For good measure she also spreads the Holy Water throughout the yard and on both the back and front porches of her home. It as at this point when she also sprinkles Hawaiian Salt on each side of the doors. Traditionally Hawaiians use Alaea salt in various ceremonies to cleanse and to purify, as well as in healing rituals for medicinal purposes.

Alaea is the traditional Hawaiian table salt used to season and preserve. Alaea Hawaiian Sea Salt is non-processed and rich in trace minerals, all of which are found within the seawater. A small amount of harvested reddish Hawaiian clay, 'Alaea, also enriches the salt with Iron Oxide.

She then says prayers that will usually "rest" the spirits themselves or rid the home of the undesired spirits. Her final step is the placement of TI leaves at each corner of the house, keeping one under the pillow of each family member in order to prevent any further activity. Ti leaves are from the beautiful

Ti plant, whose leaves Hawaiians believe possess healing powers and brings the bearer good luck.

When her sons went camping she was sure to give them packets of Hawaiian Salt and lots of Ti-leaves for placement in each corner of their tent, under their pillow, and one to keep on their person as well.

It is interesting to note the blending of the Catholic belief system, Holy Water and Rosary Prayer, with the Hawaiian influence, the Hawaiian Salt and Ti leaves.

This type of combined personal ritual that she has shared with us is not that which is usually practiced by modern day Catholicism, however we are told that this practice is common, with some variations, among the people of Hawaiian ancestry. We are also told of "The Gift" which she says in Hawaiian ancestry makes you hyper-sensitive to spiritual activity and communication, and is something she feels blessed to have and to share with us.

As they say on the Island, "Mahalo", which means *thank you*, as we do feel greatly indebted to this very kind woman for sharing her history, her insight, and her beliefs of the afterlife with us.

The above image is of a Hawaiian Ti plant and comes in both red and green leaves. Photo taken by Laurie Medeiros from the island of Kaua'i in 2009.

The Voice of the Peruvian Medium

Peru is quite a remarkable country and very memorable as it was the first country Barry experienced an earth tremor. An experience that made him climb out of bed in the hotel get dressed and climb back into bed as his belief was if a larger earthquake was to hit he was going to be dressed as a gentleman when they found him in the rubble rather than drag his naked ass out of a pile of dirt with the worlds cameras watching.

Dustin labeled the country 'Beep Beep Peru' due to the seemingly unusual population's pastime of beeping the horn whilst driving along the roads which is littered with thousands of vehicles. Many times there is no reason to beep, it seems to be a subconscious comfort reaction. But soon Barry too was beeping the car horn in respect to the countries pastime.

But a Catholic practicing medium offered his thoughts on the dilemma this book brought about in regards ridding the house of troublesome spirits. South America seems to be a place very open to ghostly phenomenon as we discovered in Argentina and of course Brazil which still holds a large part of our hearts.

The medium, although Catholic, finds an affinity with the Protestant Evangelical Church but was not perturbed by the two distinct perspectives of the Christian faith.

He went on to say that both the Protestant and Catholic appreciations for the spirit world have always been identified by him stating, *'both the Protestants and Catholics always wise of this world since the creation especially in the life beyond.'*

It seemed from the interview that the treatment awarded to the spirit was very much reflective on the nature of the spirit being positive or negative.

He believed a home or location could become haunted because the departed soul may have some unfinished business on the earth plane and will manifest in the spirits former home or the departed may have simply become lost and require help to locate the light.

This concept of returning to the light can be found in most major cultures around the world and is a phenomenon which can be found in nearly all the hospitals of the world as patients have reported dying which is supported by medical facts and seeing a wonderful light that inspires peace and a heightened level of love. In his book 'Going Home' Irish journalist Colm Keane describes many cases of near death experiences which have occurred in Ireland and he has painstakingly collected the stories of those that have died and returned to tell the living of their experiences with a shocking similarity.

In the Peruvian mediums case he believed that if a home became disturbed he would try and develop a bridge with the spirit allowing him the ability to receive messages from the disturbed spirit in an attempt to resolve the situation and help the spirit back on its course to the light without it attaching itself to him, which for obvious reasons would be a good example of the need not to bring your work home with you.

But when he was asked once the spirit was released and the home was quiet once again and it returned what would his course of action be, he stated that this has never happened to him before as his gift has been successful to this point.

Africa

A brief history lesson.

Africa holds the handsome title of being the second largest continent as well as the second largest populated land mass beaten of course only by Asia. Its growing population of over a billion people have stemmed from extinct cultures swallowed by sands and jungle producing a vast array of beliefs and customs.

At approximately 3300 BC history started to record events in ancient and very successful Egypt located in Northern Africa. Before Europe's intervention in African affairs there were approximately 10,000 different cultures throughout the continent.

The Arab slave trade stole a record 18 million slaves from Africa and taken through the trans-Saharan and Indian Ocean routes. Of course the more famous Atlantic slave trade between the fifteenth and the nineteenth centuries, took up to 12 million slaves to the New World until its decline in the 1820's.

Anti-slavery legislation in Europe and America finally forced the remaining nails in the coffin toward this barbaric habit and with the British Royal Navy's help between 1808 and 1860, they seized nearly 1,600 slave ships freeing 150,000 Africans.

The Continent of Africa

The continent of Africa is still a land of travels we sought out some natives who could speak about the old traditions of the tribes and how they have held onto the importance of ancestry yet also have embraced some new ideas. But we are still left feeling disturbed by acts of great harm and even death caused by superstition in Africa. It has been reported on multiple occasions on reprehensible behaviour sparked by some tribe's witch doctors and superstitious beliefs which was once common place in Europe. But in Africa some beliefs for instance support the idea of raping a young child to death which is claimed will cure the perpetrators of aids. Burning men, women and children or running them from their homes still occur if they believe them to be witches and are accused of manipulating the dark arts.

Human sacrifice although not as common these days sadly still does occur and some of these practices are traveling with immigrants as they seek better lives all over the world. Take for instance the case of Adam in London, it involved a dismembered body found in the river Thames which flows past the UK's main government seat, the Houses of Parliament, made famous by the huge clock 'Big Ben'.

On the afternoon of Friday 21 September 2001 a human torso was seen floating in the great river, the alarm was raised and the Metropolitan Police

Service retrieved the remains from the water. After a post-mortem the remains were believed to have belonged to a young boy between the ages of four and seven. As there was no other identifying marks to the remains he became known as 'Adam'. The post-mortem uncovered the amount of British food in Adam's stomach and pollen in his lungs indicating he had only been in the United Kingdom for a few days, but a potion containing ingredients used in African ritual magic was also discovered in his stomach.

Adam soon developed into a mystery, but his bones were analyzed by science to see if they could determine his geographical origins. Apparently everything a person eats bears the trace of the soil of where it was grown or reared and using these advanced tests it was determined that Adam originated in the Yoruba Plateau in Nigeria, Africa.

Despite the Metropolitan police force traveling to Nigeria and launching a campaign to track Adam's parents little was ever discovered and the killers were never captured.

During the publication of this work we discovered much the same as the police when searching for information on ritual magic as no one wants to talk and it can simply disappear.

London strangely enough is also one of those places you will find the 'Marabout', originally Muslim holy mean that walked through Africa, peace makers and advisers on spiritual matters but in the

UK has evolved into the practice of witchcraft offering various amulets to fix problems as well as offering powerful spells to counteract any form of witchcraft you feel or rather they feel you suffer from. At a price.

Houses of Parliament on the banks of the river Thames in London, England. Picture by Barry FitzGerald.

An apple a day keeps the Witch Doctor at bay.

The influence of witchdoctors on the public mindset in Africa should not be underestimated; murder, sacrifice and cannibalism are growing in some African countries, mostly for reasons of power and greed. Reports have been leaking out of the continent and these are quite disturbing and horrific. But this dark side of the supernatural should not be ignored for hope that it goes away, it is by acknowledging it and getting behind the public awareness and making our voice heard that we may hopefully break the back of these horrifying acts and get behind worldwide campaigns calling for it to end. Of course we have already touched on the body in the River Thames in the United Kingdom but let's take it right back to Africa, what is happening there yesterday, today and disturbingly, tomorrow.

A report in the Fortean Times dated April 2010 describes a young Albino girl who turned up murdered on the Kenyan, Tanzanian border just outside a town called Isebania. This was unlike the usual case or murder as body parts had been removed. The chairman of the Albino association of Kenya, Issac Mwaura said 90% of Albino in the region are raised by single mothers as the fathers accuse them of having affairs with white men. Albinos suffer from a hereditary condition when both parents donate a recessive gene. There people in Africa are seen by some followers as having unnatural powers, supernatural powers, much like those born with red hair who on some occasions are sacrificed when entering puberty. Andrew Malone from the Daily Mail in the United Kingdom said many Africans believe that having sex with an albino will cure diseases, a belief that has led to countless rapes leaving the victim HIV positive.

The Zulu word *muti* simply refers to medicine, however it is widely used throughout Africa by numerous other African languages and now is referred to as medicine murders but the African police service and sociologists as it can also refer to supernatural medicine. But the staggering fact of this act is that during the process of removing the parts required for muti the victim must be conscious. It is believed that during the mutilation the agonizing screams of the victim makes the muti more potent before they succumb to shock and blood loss. Most of the recent escalation in albino attacks has happened since 2000 with the attack of 20 year old Enicko Simkolo who was clubbed as he worked in a remote field and skinned alive, his skin which was valued at $5000 US. The list goes on and on. But the police in Tanzania, Malawi and Zambia have taken action and expelled any foreign witch doctors blamed for the skin trade.

In November 2009 figures released by the International Federation of the Red Cross and Cresent Societies (IFRCCS) had shown that at least 44 albinos were killed in Tanzania and 14 in Burundi the preceding year.

In a month before the report a 10 year old albino boy, Gasper Elikana, was beheaded and his leg chopped off in an attack that also left his father severely injured. The IFRCCS report added that a complete set of albino body parts (limbs, genitals, eyelids, ears, tongue, nose and even skin) can fetch around $75,000 US and it's no wonder there is a growing anxiety among albinos throughout Africa. Due to this more than 10,000 have already been displaced and went into hiding.

However despite the crackdown in July 2009 around 200 people were arrested including a man at the border with an albino baby's head on his person. Despite 100 people on death row associated with these crimes said a local BBC correspondent no one has been executed in 15 years and the muti murders continue.

Chilling.

A similar report in the Paranormal Magazine in March 2010 quoted BBC special correspondent Tim Whewell as he talked about his firsthand accounts of child sacrifice in Uganda.

The Ugandan Government have confirmed child sacrifice is on the increase as folks try to get rich and people believe that killing children can help and it should be noted that sometimes these are their own children. Some capture other people's children and bring the heart and blood to the witchcraft ceremony.

One former witch doctor commented that it's not unusual for people to arrive at a ceremony with various body parts and blood, probably about 3 times a week. Before converting to Christianity one Witchdoctor openly admitted to killing over 70 children is sacrifice rituals.

In neighboring Kenya it has grown in popularity as well, but since the quoted witchdoctor's conversion to Christianity in 1990 he has managed to convert 2400 others from the practice of ritual magic.

Uganda's Minister of Ethics and Integrity James Nsaba Buturo believes that 'to punish retrospectively would cause a problem...if we can persuade Ugandans to change this is much better than going back into the past and hence it is not likely people will be charged if they have stopped the practice.

But the continent of Africa is rich in culture and history which outstrips Europe by thousands of years and it was during a trip to South Africa we I had the pleasure to chat with some of the Zulu nation.

Standing proud for they are Zulu.

The proud Zulu tribe is the largest ethnic group in South Africa. They believe that they are descendents from a chief within the Congo area, and in the 16th century migrated to the South African region. We had the distinct pleasure to meet with them on one of our travels in 2008 and were pleased to explore the Zulu culture that is just one example of the beautiful and yet deadly land of Africa.

Their belief system is very similar to a high proportion of western culture for the most part. They believe the body, called *umZimba*, is directly linked to the spirit, called *iDlozi*. Both live with each other throughout the human life, but the iDlozi is the only part to exist once the umZimba is struck by the cold hand of death which we all must face, (well not Barry as he has a hibernation tank which runs on AA batteries and intends to live forever, or at least until the $10 he leaves in his will to replace the batteries every few days runs out). The Zulu belief that the IDlozi or spirit lives on is similar to the idea in western society about the afterlife in regards to the soul.

The amaDlozi, or ancestor spirits who have passed on, are seen to be helpful and for the most part benign. But they can become troublesome and may indeed become harmful if neglected and forgotten about, thus the people of the Zulu tribe continue to respect their elders long after they have passed.

The Zulu use various techniques to contact their ancestors and believe that such contact may come to them in the form of dreams, omens, and varying ceremonies that can be conducted by a spiritual healer, or the blunt label given to them by the West is "Witch Doctor".

The Zulu believe that the ancestral spirit may select a person to become the new spiritual healer for the tribe and to turn it down has been known to cause madness in the person.

There are no fancy pieces of equipment necessary for any of these ceremonies; it's simply felt emotionally and spiritually and may also include ceremonial offerings. Similar sense of feeling is known in the Christian belief system as God would draw close to ask them to do something or inspire them to move in a particular path and less we forget the modern medium who converse with spirit in much the same way. The Zulu believe that spirit manifestation can occur on many occasions, similar to the old English medium, but set in less stringent parameters.

The modern Christian Zulu has a strong connection to the ancestral spirit that they still cling to despite the disapproval of the Church and the subsequent attempts to destroy that connection and for the most part have been successful as most Zulu Christians will no longer consult diviners to the spiritual realm.

But with that said it is still interesting to see that even in the westernization of the Zulu traditional belief system and religious practices, that the bond between the ancestors and the living, along with the respect for those in the spirit world remains strong despite the churches best efforts.

Hoodoo voodoo, chooka chooky choo choo.

The West African coastline is a place stepped in magic and myth, known once as the Slave Coast because it was the hub of the transatlantic slave trade for several centuries.

In Africa, Voodoo simply means spirit. However Voodoo in Christianity's eyes has been labeled as a black magic cult, but really in truth Voodoo is used for healing and helping people.

In the West African nations of Benin, Togo and Ghana, Voodoo is widely practiced. But Voodoo is not really different from any other religion, there are good and bad in all religions. However we are not aware of heads of animals being used for rituals of superstition found in any other religion, but we do display relics of Saints bones and such and we should not be quick to throw that first stone.

Owls and vultures heads for instance are used in Voodoo to counteract bad curses placed on you by a Botono who practices Bo a dark side of Voodoo. Hexes are not placed on people by those that practice Voodoo, but rather a sorcerer who dapples (*dabbles) in Bo.

Voodoo of course can and has been abused because of Botono much like Satanic worship is in Christianity. It has been recognized that Voodoo is entrenched deep in the earth of West Africa and it not easy to shift and even though there is a type of spiritual warfare going on at the moment with Protestant evangelists they are having a tough time as some that are converting to Christianity are once again returning to Voodoo, or Vodun as known in the French regions of the African continent. In the Spanish speaking ports and plantations found in countries such as Cuba a form of Voodoo developed called Santeria.

In America there is another form of magic practiced apply called Hoodoo which is a mixture of Voodoo brought from New Orleans and other French plantation sites in the USA and mixed with the Native American belief systems.

Its first documentation was in 1827 and unlike Voodoo which is a practice of religion Hoodoo is simply a collection of magical rites and should not be mistaken for Voodoo.

Rituals within voodoo ceremonies are as highly structured as those of any Western church and has been suggested human sacrifices in West Africa have ended a century ago. However it has not totally gone away.

Much like the human sacrifices linked to Satanic practices in the USA and Europe. But like the witches of old in Europe the use of drugs are vital in winning over their follows, take for instance one case in Jamaica where a spell of wasting disease was placed on the subject, who really did waste away to nothing and died a horrible death. However it was discovered powdered glass was being placed in his food which produced this predicted end.

A spokes person in Jamaica who we spoke to stated that Obeah (Obi) he believed was indeed one of the truest forms of the native spiritual belief system in the Caribbean unlike the practice found in former French colonies in Haiti and New Orleans for example called Voodoo. But in truth its history is hard to follow as many will not talk to those wishing to know more and many will claim their respective guides will not allow the knowledge to be written about.

Most of the slaves imported from the African West coast to Jamaica came from Ghana and most were from the Ashanti tribes which were known as one of the most spiritual of all the tribes in West Africa.

There are other locations where this form of religious worship can be seen such as Trinidad & Tobago in the southern Caribbean.

Obi priests have been known to be very secretive and we certainly seen this continuation of mystery in Jamaica leading to rumor and of course missleading facts presented to us through our television screens.

Obeah in its truest form is a practice which is neither positive nor negative, but its intention is wielded by the priest that conjures it. But within Obi practices there are lighter forms of sorcery known as Mialism and is used to counteract the darker nature of Obi. Duppy are spirits/ghost of people which are conjured by the high priest to inflict harm or be inspired to help someone. In Trinidad and Tobago we see the use of Jumbie, a type of evil spirit and has been suggested that this is the origins of the zombie but we believe that is more evident in the Haitian and Puerto Rican cultures of Voodoo as particular chemicals taken from the Puffer fish are utilized to immobilize the subject by collapsing the central nervous system. However should a sorcerer use Duppy to intimidate a person the activity can arrive in the night hours and can take the form of stone throwing on the persons home. In some accounts the amount of stones thrown in a night will come very fast and from all directions and in the morning the subject's home will look like a small quarry site.

But we were both surprised to learn that the Catholic Priest is seen as the biggest threat to the Obi priest as they believe he holds greater strength and can destroy the powerful advances of the Obi magic. Obi is tied on the island with the Spiritual Baptist practices, a protestant branch of Christianity and on some occasions you may find some elements of Obi being used in one of the services and vice versa. Obi practices it has been claimed have also found its

way into some parts of the Muslim faith within the islands of the Caribbean.

Voodoo however has more association with Catholicism as particular Saints used in Christian services are utilized during Voodoo ceremonies, but it should be noted here that during slavery it had to be practiced this way to safe guard the people participating in the ceremony.

These native ceremonies were frowned upon by plantation owners and the slaves had to be seen as accepting the Christian ideals. So in order to cover their tracks they used the Christian Saints as a front to call on their own Loa and have them renamed.

The Loa are almost akin to angels and are seen as the messengers to God, but unlike angels whom most Christians would have a quick word with on a daily or weekly basis the Loa are served with each having their own identity, their own symbols, songs and rituals.

Within Voodoo there is a belief in a ritual that takes place one year and one day after the death of a deceased relative, within the belief system it recognizes two parts to the human soul. These are the ti-bon-ange meaning little good angel and gros-bon-ange meaning great good angel. After death, the gros-bon-ange has to return to the cosmos but to ensure the ti-bon-ange is at a peaceful rest, the gros-bon-ange must be summoned through an elaborate expensive ritual involving the sacrifice of a large animal to appease the ti-bon-ange. If the ti-bon-ange spirit is not satisfied its spirit can remain trapped on earth forever and bring illness or disasters to others.

Within these belief systems they believe that when we are weakened through a death or an illness we must be careful as like attracts like. Depression it is believed will attract the attention of negative entities who share that same energy. It is believed that such entities would be keen to keep you in that frame of mind and they must be cleared either from the home or the person. Obi does recognize like its cousin Voodoo that not only property can become troubled by negative spirit but so can our bodies.

By taking a bath is salt water or swimming in natural water such as a lake in the waning moon is seen as a good way of cleansing spirits from our auras that have become attached.

These ritual baths should be done completely naked and all the time whilst swimming asking the water spirits to
remove the negative attachments, once you feel the situation has changed you should then leave the water and thank the spirits for their help and get dressed unless you like to make a scene and get yourself arrested for behavior not fitting for a lady or gentleman and end up on a list somewhere on the internet.

There are other ways to banish entities from your home using the methods described to us in these native African religions but should only be practiced by those that are aware of the dangers involved and be versed in these techniques. Bathing in water is one thing but expelling demons is quite another. If you decide to go swimming as mentioned in the technique above then bring a trusted friend with you to make sure you are not swimming with crocodiles in Lake Placid, that could turn out messy.

Australia

A brief history lesson.

Australia is the largest island in the world covering 7.5 million square kilometers. Its variable landscapes of natural beauty don't only exist on land for if you ever have the chance to dive during your visit to this huge island we would recommend you do so on the Great Barrier Reef, a massive bed of coral which lies off the north-east coast and extends for over 2,000 kilometers.

Before European intervention in Australian affairs in the 18th century the lands inhabitance of Aboriginal people and Torres Strait Islanders lived there for about 40,000 years and where made up of 250 individual nations but currently now only make up 2.6% of Australia's modern population.

The Tasmanian Aborigines located on the island of Tasmania off Australia's south east coast had a population estimated as high as 6,000 people but were reduced to around 300 between 1803 and 1833 due to introduced diseases and the callous actions of the British settlers which we learned about whilst on a visit to Tasmania with the obvious result of having their numbers completely wiped out on the island.

The English explorer James Cook named the area of New South Wales in Australia and claimed it for Great Britain. His work set the footing for the establishment of the infamous penal colonies absorbing thousands from all over the great English

Empire setting the corner stone's for a new history of this huge landmass.

Australia as you have read is huge and a land full of spirits. The native peoples of this continent are well versed in their spiritual awareness but what about the cultures that were introduced to it? Is it possible they brought some of their own spirits to this land? The following is an account kindly told by one of the countries residents and is a tale with striking similarities to those entities found in Europe or the USA, it reads:

I lay restless in my bed, my husband sleeping soundly by my side. Glancing over to my cell phone I read 2:34AM. To try and kick start my sleep time I decided to listen to some music on my iPod with the hope that I would eventually drift off. I popped in my earphones and wriggled away to a hip hop tune on the bed.

However, amidst my wriggling my elbow bumped into what felt like someone standing next to the bed beside me, opening my eyes I looked up and caught a glimpse of a shadow of a person towering over me. I jolted upright on the bed, awakening my husband at the same time. Perhaps he felt something was up and asked me "What's wrong? What's wrong?" I was unable to reply immediately because my eyes kept scanning the bedroom, seeking out for a shadow or movement. Again my husband asked, "What's wrong love?" "There's someone in our bedroom!" I said out loud.

My husband turned on his bedside lamp. Naturally, no one was there. Our bedroom door was closed, and we didn't hear anyone opening the door to go out but I still felt there was a presence in the room. My husband pulled me towards him in a hug "Just pray love." We prayed Our Father and my husband turned off his lamp.

A few moments passed by and my eyes adjusted to the darkness in the room. I then saw the shadow again, standing, on my husbands' side of the bed. I screamed out and clung onto my husband. He turned the lamp on again and of course, no one was there.

The emotions that was running through me at that time, were somewhat mixed, but I believe I was more scared than anything else. But what scared me the most was what happened next...

"Jesus Jesus Jesus, cover us Lord with your most precious blood." My husband kept on chanting it, repeating it. A prayer that he uses whenever something bad was happening or about to happen. In the meantime, I was clinging on to him like my life depended on it and I was glad that I did.

Suddenly, something or someone grabbed me by the ankle, and tugged at my feet. I screamed, "It touched me! It touched me! It touched me!" My husband kept reassuring me that there was no one there. With the lamp still on, I looked towards the bottom of the bed and saw a face of a child. I didn't tell my husband this, but the child looked as real as if he was alive, but his little face looked somewhat contorted. I just closed my eyes, curled my feet up under me, buried my face into my husband's chest and chanted with him, "Jesus Jesus Jesus, cover us Lord with your most precious blood..."

After what seemed like forever, I opened my eyes and looked around the bedroom. No signs of the child or shadows and for some reason I felt somewhat silly after making a big fuss like that. I don't know how, but somehow, I managed to drift off to sleep soon after. It was an experience but something I wouldn't wish to happen again.

Thankfully our friend in Australia was only visited the once, but this once will be etched in her mind for as long as she lives. These experiences can be equally shocking as thrilling, depending on the situation and entity. Many times these experiences occur as these bodiless forms pass through our homes to a destination maybe they are even unaware of. But let's have a look at native culture in Australia and understand in part how they would deal with such a situation should the entity decide to stay longer than welcome.

The Paranormal Down Under

Upon the continent of Australia and its territories there are various understandings of the spirit world at work, depending on if you are an Aussie, a Tazzie, or a member of the Native Aboriginal People. It was here that we realised how difficult a situation some populations around the world are having with their cultures and having to hold on to their social identities. Take for instance in Australia they have lost over 120 languages in the past century, a number which is similarly seen in Brazil located in South America. But we did have the opportunity to meet a few people who were very keen to have their voices heard and appreciated.

Australia's disappearing Aboriginal Culture

Our belief system is based on The Dreaming and our spiritual relationship with the land. The Dream time explains the origins of the universe, the continuous cycle of life and our links with our Spirit Ancestors.

Although there are over 400 different cultural groups, The Dreaming is the only traditional religious experience practiced by Aboriginal people. The names of our Spirit Ancestors will vary but the belief system remains the same. I have practiced this way of life since I was born.

The Dream time tells us about the Creation time when our Spiritual Ancestors, who had supernatural powers, created Dreaming places and all living things. These Ancestors could turn into animal or human form whenever they wanted. They created the landscape and gave life to our Mother Earth. The Legends of the Dream time have been handed down from generation to generation for over 60,000 years or since time began. As there was no written language, these Dreaming stories were told through the visual and performing arts. Special ceremonies were performed by each community to give blessing to the Ancestors and our Spiritual Mother Earth and these ceremonies are still performed today.

There are many different types of Spirits within our belief system. There are protecting Spirits that look after our children and teach them right from wrong. There are cheeky Spirits that are "naughty" and cause small accidents and there are bad Spirits that bring bad fortune and sickness. We have special individual ceremonies that relate to each Spirit.

There are many places that become haunted. Since 1770, many of our Sacred Sites have been built on or destroyed.
Places may become haunted for different reasons. One is because bad things might have happened at that place or a person is not doing the right thing by their culture. Or there are good Spirits that look

after us, like the Spirits of our family or our Totems. I have known of cases where people have dug up sacred objects and kept them in their homes. Even after the object has been taken out and given back to the community, bad Spirits stay around to cause trouble.

I have been involved in a situation where the house had troublesome spirits. I contacted a person to perform a special ceremony to Smoke out the bad Spirits. The place now has good Spirits and the people are happy with the outcome. They don't feel afraid anymore. If the bad Spirit came back again, I would talk to one of our Elders about performing a stronger ceremony. In the majority of cases, the Smoking ceremony is enough.

No Religious Affiliation in Tasmania

We were told that in Tasmania Christianity dominates the Religious landscape, with a smattering of Buddhism. The woman we spoke with in Tasmania was raised an Anglican but currently does not affiliate herself with any organized Religion. She has chosen to take her belief systems out of the Church and simply tries to live her life being a good person and doing no harm to others.

She says that in regards to Tasmania religion is growing less important than in other parts of the world. She reports seeing a growing interest among the younger generations towards Paganism and getting back to nature. The older population remains more conservative and structured in their beliefs but the youth movement is largely more alternative. Mostly the younger generations are looking into Gothic life styles, embracing Paganism and to a much lesser extent she has also witnessed those practicing Satanism. Religious affiliation as a whole has become shattered and secularized by sub communities. Interestingly enough, the media and its portrayal of religious ideals seem to be heavily influencing the youth movement in their views of both faith and the paranormal.

In regards to a dwelling becoming haunted the popular theory remains that of a sudden loss of life, or a death under tragic circumstances.

Suicides top the list as to why someone would linger in this world, as well as unfinished business that the spirit feels a need to communicate.

The paranormal is not something that is openly discussed. It appears that avoidance of discussion in regards to all things paranormal is what you will commonly come across in Tasmania. There seems to exist a complicated construct around death and spirits and that the society itself is not too comfortable speaking about it.

Again there seems to be a divide between the generations. We are told that the younger generation is more open-minded than the older generation, but they remain skeptical none the less.

Technology speaks volumes to the people of Tasmania that are interested in the paranormal. They do not hold psychics
in very high regard and this they say is due to media portrayal of the archetypical "séance psychic".
The local Catholic Church views of paranormal research has been quite restrictive and will only involve themselves if they feel its warranted, and even these are not the mainstream churches but rather some offshoots and subdivisions.

Some local paranormal groups perform cleansings, however they note that the effectiveness of the cleansing is dependent upon the belief system of the homeowner versus the belief system of the person doing the cleansing, we already have come across this thought process with the American Southern Baptist representative on earlier pages. A typical cleansing ritual involves opening a spiritual connection, the opening of a doorway from a higher spirit who is
then asked to lead out the restless spirit of the one left behind. This is often done via the use of ancient languages, by which the person doing the

cleansing asks the higher spirit to lead the troubled spirit to the afterlife.

If the lingering spirits do not wish to leave they are simply left behind, they cannot be forced onwards, only enticed to move forth and encouraged to travel on. She likens it to "psychic social working", in effect trying to match up the wrestles spirit with the right higher entity to go home with.

It was eye opening to see the divide between the generations and the influence that media has upon the beliefs and practices of the young. A sharp reminder to all those in the limelight about how vast their influence can be, and how much responsibility goes along with publicity. May we all remember that in all walks of life, we all set an example for someone, and it is imperative that example be one of honesty and respect.

Europe

A brief history lesson

Haven traveled extensively throughout Europe it is hard to comprehend that is in fact the world's second smallest continent by surface area. But if you ever have the pleasure to travel throughout the wonderful states of Europe you may eventually find yourself stumbling into one of the smallest countries in Europe. Hidden inside Rome, Italy you will find the Vatican City and although small is certainly one of the richest countries in the world.

But even though Europe is small it certainly is well populated and is the third most populated continent after Asia and Africa, with a population climbing in numbers over 7 million. The earliest evidence of life in the European region lived roughly 1.8 million years ago in Georgia now inside controversial Russian control and later remains have been located in Germany and Spain.

In Europe's early development it was ravaged by war, more so since the weakening of the great Roman Empire controlled from Rome, Italy which thrust Europe into the Dark Ages. Tribes migrated and some isolated Monasteries where able to keep limited records which shed some light on this rather unusual time.

Since the collapse of the Russian Soviet Union in 1991 to the east of its boarders Europe has expanded uniting the countries of Poland, Romania etc, etc with the European Union and now rests against the Russian boarders much to the annoyance of the Russian leaders who occasionally have their huge bombers escorted out of European airspace.

Over the centuries Europe's development continued and the last war on its boarders became known as the Yugoslavian wars which started in 1991 turning out to be one of the most embarrassing moments in Europe's modern history. Strangely enough casualty figures are hard to come by even in these modern times, but an example of the barbarism that occurred was uncovered with a mass grave being found in Kosovo in 1999 with over 2000 bodies.

But it's most notable wars happened in WW1 1914-18 & WW2 1939-45 with the casualty figures estimated above 37 million men, women and children.

The German roller coaster in 20th century took the world on a harrowing trip which seen the loss of many lives and the attempted extermination of several races of people from Europe. Approximately 6 million Jews and gypsies lost their lives in Europe during WW2 alone, whilst on the Russian boarder Stalin, the Russian leader was clocking the death count at 21 million defending Russia from the Nazi advance.

European Vacation

The old world with all of its history, majestic castles and countless stories is a land full of spirit activity and different approaches to it.

We start our journey at the enchanting and lovely land of Ireland with her green hillsides and pristine landscapes. (And we do not just say that because it is home to Mr. Fitzgerald)

The Pagan Witches of Ireland

We were fortunate enough to have been granted an interview from two very knowledgeable modern witches located on the Emerald Isle whom have been practicing the Wiccan ways for over a combined 55 years. We think it would be prudent to give some more information on the Wiccan belief as it has been labeled and misjudged for a long time and we did not want our readers to me mislead by this black & white approach taken by some narrow minded people on this planet.

It has been suggested that the Wicca religion stems from an earlier Neopagan religion, it evolved quite abruptly in England in the early 20th century from the bones of the early pagan beliefs into what we know it as today, and in truth and in reflection Christianity followed the same evolutionary path to develop into what we know and practice today. For those that would object simply think about this question, would the early pilgrims and teachers of Christianity from 2000 years ago recognize the faith as they did? This goes for all the major religions. Wicca was brought into the public focus in the 1950's by Gerald Gardner, a retired British civil servant, who labeled it the 'witch cult'.

Wiccans worship a recognized Goddess and God and include the ritual use of magic and the celebration of eight seasonally based festivals. Controversy was rife in its development in the 1950's and one of Gardner's rivals, Charles Cardell based it on the Old English word Wicca, which referred to male practitioners of sorcery.

Traditionally the God is viewed as a Horned God, associated with nature, wilderness, sexuality and hunting and was known by various names such as Cernunnos, Pan, Atho and Karnayna, the early depiction of Pan is very similar to the Christian belief of the Devil and may indeed be just that as an emerging religion will alienate the old gods. According to Gerald Gardner, the deities of Wicca are prehistoric gods of the British Isles. Modern scholarship has cast doubt on this claim; however various different horned gods and mother goddesses were worshiped in the British Isles in the ancient and early medieval periods.

But modern day Wiccans voiced their opinions on the questions we asked for this book and we are grateful to be able to include their voices in this publication.

They tell us of their firm belief in a spirit realm, where various spirits and their ability to interact with them is an essential part of the Wiccan theology and worldview. They believe in different 'level's' of reality where different spirit forms reside.

These spirits are regarded and treated with respect. Nature spirits, elemental forms. In early Greek belief systems and beliefs that followed the elemental understanding was a basic belief of fundamental building blocks within nature. There were four elements: earth, water, air and fire. From this came the belief and understanding of mythological beings identifying them as belonging to one of the four elemental types.

Gnomes and such like belonged to earth elemental structure of nature which included fairies and similar. Undines belonged to the water structure of elementals and are extremely dangerous if caution is not aired when dealing with them. Sylphs and such like are of course air elementals whilst the natural hot headed salamanders were seen to belong to the fire elements, whilst they are hard to control due to their reluctance to take orders, they were seen by old pagan practitioners as being useful during a siege situation which were called upon and sent into a building to burn it from the inside out.

The elementals are considered to be an intrinsic part of the natural order of things. Other spirits e.g. discarnate entities, individuals who have been unable to move on to their next incarnation after death, are believed to require healing by the Wiccan practitioners to do this.

Though there is a distinction between positive and negative influences within their beliefs, it is important to note that a negative influence is normally considered to be an imbalance rather than 'evil' in the Judeo-Christian worldview sense. A negative spirit influence, e.g. a 'negative' discarnate spirit that has attached itself to someone and is causing problems, we believe requires assistance to 'move on' rather than any form of exorcism.

It is their understanding that there exists different ways by which a home may become haunted. The first is that there is an etheric recording of an incident of violence that has taken place. This is no more than a recording, which is replayed under certain circumstances. (What we would refer to as a *residual* type.) The second reason for a haunting is a discarnate entity, a person who does not know they are dead and is kicking up at having 'intruders' in their home. The third is poltergeist activity; normally associated with adolescent teenagers; and the fourth is elemental activity. A house may be built on a negative lay (black stream) or 'fairy path', a place known for it's elemental spirit activity. They have personally witnessed all four of these types of haunting's over the years, having been called out to 'clear' the properties. Barry was intrigued as they told him a story about cattle committing suicide by drowning themselves on a particular site in Ireland and how they had to calm the elemental spirits by making them an offering and establishing peace. It seemed to work as the farmer no longer has any problems with his cattle on that piece of land.

A very similar problem raised its head in Switzerland in the European Union in 2009. The country known for exquisite chocolate, banks, assisted suicide for those with no hope of survival from terminal illness and a deep routed hatred for noisy cars was reported by a well established UK newspaper to have dozens of cows in the Swiss village of Lauterbrunnen appear to commit suicide without any assistance unlike their human counterparts..

In just three days, 28 cows and bulls had thrown themselves from a cliff and no doubt becoming mince meat as they abruptly arrived at their deaths on the rocks hundreds of meters below.

Investigating police remained baffled as they stated cows growing up in the mountains normally identify dangers and do not plunge from cliffs. They went on to say it was extremely rare for Alpine cows to die in falls. When spirits become troublesome and they are called in to help, what they do really depends on the circumstances of the case. But the first stage is always an assessment of cause to define what is going on and why it is happening.

This includes an account of the reported activity itself along with the noted history of the property, and a list of whom is living there, e.g. adolescents in the house and so forth.

The next stage is communication with the entity in an effort to try and discover it's intent and how it can be 'helped'. Once this in understood and all the factors have been taken into consideration, only then do they move on to the third stage, which is 'clearing'. How this takes place depends on the cause of the activity, but in the case of a discarnate entity (a genuine haunting) it would consist of a séance to help the spirit pass-over. In the case of an elemental form, you would need to appease it in some form as it will feel that it's 'territory' has been invaded. In some cases it might be necessary to use dowsing and copper nails or similar to re-route a 'fairy path', a line of elemental energy.

The final stage is to make sure that any negative influences once gone are replaced with positive ones and the individuals and property are 'protected'. In Wicca there is a traditional circle casting method that includes the calling of elemental guardians we would use, but again, the methodused would really depend on the cause. We would normally check up and re-asses a few weeks later.

Dustin and I are aware of a rite of exorcism which like the Christian exorcism is used by those of authority in the Wiccan community. However its premise in the USA is very different to those of the worldwide Christian. The authority figures in the Wicca system actually trap the entity in the home or location therefore the entity is not free to wander and the metaphorical noose is tightened around its neck.

There are particular verses recited in the Wiccan exorcism like those seen in the Rites of Exorcism used by Rome, but unlike the versions from the vaults of the Vatican it is thought that they don't need to be learnt by the letter. Dustin and I like the Wiccans believe that it is the intent and the nature of the gesture which is more important than anything else. So if you fluffed your lines you will still be grand as long as your concentration and confidence in the task at hand are not damaged.

After the exorcism the householder should be aware there may be a time of disturbance which follows over the subsequent 24 hours but this is not because the exorcism failed but rather it is believed the energy in the house is readjusting and really should be nothing to fear.

However there is an air of warning that even though the activity will have stopped and the previous disturbances are at rest the home owner and family should not dwell on the past activity which may have been traumatic but should release those thoughts and not even talk about them. It is believed that by doing so may indeed draw them back and that's the last thing the family needs so leave it buried so to speak.

Christianity's view point

Christianity although now split into many subdivisions does try to remain true to its core values. Since its split due mostly to the teachings of the German reformer Martin Luther in the 16th century the Protestant faith has taken a different view point and its approach to spirits is somewhat indecisive as some preachers and ministers of the faith will deny the existence, or some will say they are all demons and even utilize a watered down version of exorcism called deliverance, whilst others will recognize it.

Within Catholicism however the belief is still strong even since the Vatican's attempts to address the issue.

For someone who shared a strong faith it has been suggested that an intercessory prayer would be required. This is a prayer designed to ask God to enter the immediate area and remove the evil spirits and can be utilized by the home owner without the help of the church, of course depending on the strength of their faith.

This is problematic as the Church has been crippled by law suits for various reasons and its reluctance to address the problems people might face in their homes due to paranormal activity will for the most part be ignored or at least show a reluctance to do anything about it and may in fact be a reflection on the faith of the practicing clergy as it's a strong faith that is required in this particular approach that will determine the success of the exorcism.

It is a common observation that exorcisms and blessings are failing faster than ever before and I just can't help but wonder if this is a true reflection of the inner belief of the church representative. It is quite possible this maybe the case, but of course we are brought back to reflect on the warnings given to us by the followers of Wicca, that
those who have suffered should not dwell on the past or even talk about them or by doing so may draw them back. We can see the rise of popularity in the paranormal within the west and of course with every story another person offers their experience and this itself may be the cause of the failures of the exorcisms as families fail to let go.

However the fact that exorcisms fail is no reflection on the Christian belief system as the same is happening the world over. Even though various followings under the umbrella of Christianity have a hard time admitting or acknowledging that there is a spirit world we can find messages for such in the Bible.
"For our struggle is not against flesh and blood, but against the rulers, against the authorities, against the powers of this dark world and against the

spiritual forces of evil in the heavenly realms."
(Eph. 6:12).

In early Christianity there always has been a belief
in the spiritual world, but for some reason I'm still
having trouble deciphering some leaders in this
faith will almost plant their head in the sand and
ignore it, hoping that it will go away. Which is not
entirely wrong as the modern media have hyped
and sensationalized the paranormal and those cries
for help from volatile individuals swayed by what
they see and hear reach to their faith for help .Time
is wasted and detracted from others but in by doing
this there is a great many families that slip through
the net who really need help and are labeled under
one heading. As one spokes person for the
Orthodox Church stated the greatest feat of the
Devil was to make people believe he did not exist,
yet another within the same believe system claimed
that evil was like a cancer, it needed a body to feed
off and destroy. 'You don't see cancer walking the
streets' he said, although true cancer does need a
body the same can be said for good and all things
positive so I didn't feel this was a good take on the
subject at hand.

But should someone find themselves in need of
help Dustin and I ask that you do something to help
yourself first. Keep a detailed diary of events.
Times and dates and of course a detailed
description of the activity. Over the course of a few

months this is quite a heavy hitting piece of proof which will help the Church or anyone else for that matter learn about the disturbances and give them a clue of what they would be dealing with or not whatever the case maybe.

We have found on occasion that the very act of keeping a diary can stop the activity from happening as writer begins to question the activity and gains more courage to explore and wonder why it happened and in that gives them strength to deal with their own knocks in the night and this can lead to the situation being dealt with inside the home.

However if the activity does continue and you have kept your diary you may wish to consult your local parish priest or minister. After a discussion with him or her we urge you to tell them everything as they need as much information as possible and this should be in the strictest of confidence. With the diary you gave them allow a few days and I'm sure you will have a blessing of your home which will settle a majority of the disturbance.

However if it does continue your local priest may have to contact the bishop of the diocese to get permission to exorcise the house and as he will have all the details at hand from the priest the likelihood of a exorcism being carried out is in your favor.

Middle East

A brief history lesson.

The Middle East blankets the areas from south west Asia and of course northern Africa and in its earlier times was more commonly known as the Near East but as it has no clear boundaries it is hard to speculate on the size of the population.

The earliest civilizations, Mesopotamia and ancient Egypt, originated in the Fertile Crescent and Nile Valley regions of Northern Africa and during the Middle East's development it has been a guiding point to many world affairs and has also boasted the origins to three major world religions known as Judaism, Christianity, and Islam.

However as many countries dotted around the Persian Gulf have huge deposits of crude oil so important to daily life and the smooth running of the other continents it has remained a sensitive region for various reasons which should be left out of this publication.

After WW1, the Middle East which was then run by the Ottoman Empire was allied with the defeated German powers and was subsequently broken into a number of separate nations. The establishment of Israel in 1948 was another transformation for the Middle Eastern social and political arena.

The mysteries of the east.

Aladdin, Ali Baba and the forty thieves, flying carpets, burning bushes and Babylonian cities the list goes on, yet all these notions are in these present days obsolete and the middle east takes on a new face. A face of gunfire, bombings and death. What has happened to the Middle East? On the ground and away from the media are the residents of the Middle East still telling stories of Sinbad to their children? Has the mystical Middle East died with thousands of its inhabitants?

We needed to find out if the mysterious east still had life in its old bones and it was of course going to be a harder task for us than ever before because we simply cannot jump on a plane and arrive on its soil and go explore, unless we wanted to make the same mistakes which were experienced in Jamaica in the Caribbean as we hunted the Obi practitioners. We had no wish to put ourselves in that type of danger again. Besides a handsome well groomed and deliciously dressed Irish man and his spiky haired American companion would find it a little tough to blend in as I like to wear my keffiyeh around my neck, not on my head and god forbid we ask Dustin to put on a hat.

First of all I thought it only fitting to examine some of the religious aspects found and practiced both in the Middle East and of course around the world.

How did people of these nations view and regard the subject of a haunted house and of course ghosts. So our initial stop off was to explore somewhat the Jewish faith and its customs.

A Jewish insight.

The Jewish history spans approximately six thousand years and encompasses hundreds of varying populations and many people who practice the Jewish faith around the world claim descent from the ancient Israelites, who originally settled in the land of Israel.

Unless you grew up under a rock you will be aware the Israelites where enslaved in Egypt by the Pharaoh usually seen as Ramses 11, but legends state that under the rule of Moses who was guided by God they escaped their oppressors and finally settled in Israel, known previously as the 'Holy Land'. This event was a profound turning point and identified the Israelites and a people. A monarchy was developed and King David's son Solomon was responsible for building the first temple in Jerusalem, but that's not all he was famous for.

Solomon was said to possess a ring which he wore that allowed him to control certain spirits. The ring it is believed was inscribed by a particular symbol garnered him control over the dreaded Jinn as spoken about in Islamic faiths. Now in modern

Israel we see a population of approximately 7.1 million people, but what of the modern belief system towards ghosts and paranormal phenomenon?

We had the opportunity to chat to a Rabbi of the Jewish faith more notably an off shoot of the Jewish faith none as Reform Judaism and we asked him some questions on this very subject and was very surprised by what he had to say. He had been practicing the Jewish faith for over 50 years and was very educated and extremely helpful in allowing us access to this ancient religion.

So we asked how the spirit world was viewed within his faith and he replied, 'You have to define a bit more precisely the "spirit world." Generally speaking, there are threads in Judaism that recognize existence of spirits (not angels or divine creatures; that's different) who play a variety of roles in our lives. The "spirit world" is an idea in Judaism, not ideology.

An interesting concept we came across was that a number of the Jewish tradition conceive that spirits were created in the twilight of creation, after mans creation but before all creation ceased. So for those spirits created after man they are caught in a limbo that is not of this realm or of the heavens and are identified somewhat as angels and others as demons.

So it was interesting to see how spirits are regarded and treated in the modern day belief system, for our speaker he said, 'It depends. For some people they are speaking with/ seeing the ghosts of loved ones who wish to speak to them. For others, spirits are kept at arm's length.

Some Jewish folklore admits a spirit has the possibility to attach itself to a living person or relative for the purposes of controlling their actions. These spirits are typically known

as a dybbuk, this term simply means clinging or cleaving. It is believed that these types of spirit will use the subject until a particular task has been completed. Unlike possession seen in Christian cases it was not believed the spirit's intent was to overtake a living creature for an unlimited period of time.

The dybbuk where not necessarily good nor evil as some were believed to have been sent to assist the living. If consulted properly with a problem it was believed a spirit who had struggled with a similar problem might respond by latching onto the individual long enough to help them. It is indeed tantalizing to think that we in the modern world would identify this will the workings of 'Spirit Guides', providing of course it had a positive outcome. But of course in the Jewish faith good and evil, positive and negative were and still are acknowledged.

But our Rabbi speaker surprised us when we asked why did he think a home would become haunted and instead of taking the road most traveled and say that it was due to a murder or some type of tragic circumstance it was quite refreshing to learn his opinion as he stated, 'Our loved ones wish to stay close or let us know that they are near to us and lovingly watching over us.'

Dustin and I were made aware of segments in the Jewish Holy Scriptures as taken from the Old Testament Hebrew to English in which spirit are mentioned and communicated with, such as 1 Samuel 16 vs 14, 'But the Spirit of the Lord departed from Saul, and an evil spirit from the Lord troubled him.' In this verse we believe describes the attachment of a spirit we would presume to be identified as a Dybbuk which attached itself to King Saul.

Another account exists in 1 Samuel 28 vs 1 - 25 which describes a typical medium induced meeting with the dead in which the spirit of the prophet Samuel is summoned and seems familiar to the old style of physical mediumship as Saul was able to talk directly to Samuel indicating he was there in some type of physical form typical to physical mediumship as seen in the old séance rooms of old.

It is recognized that should a spirit become troublesome in a home that there is an exorcism that can be carried out, it's seen though as dated and is rarely practiced these days. It seems like the Christianized form of exorcism which too is rarely practiced today day.

But when asked what course of action would one take if the entity returned he replied, 'I don't have an answer to this question. I don't know if a dybbuk can come back to a person once it has been exorcised.'

Islam and haunting's in the Middle East.

Both Dustin and I found it painfully difficult to talk to anyone of either the Hindu or Muslim faith, we even had a spokes person in the Kingdom of Bahrain and it proved difficult but not impossible.

But we did make eventual contact with the help of our wonderful spokes person and the following insight was gained from the land of mystery and magic.

Within Islam there are a number of different denominations that are for the most part similar in belief but display significant theological and legal differences. There is a big difference between the Sunni which make up 80% of the Muslim population and the Shi'a following behind with 19%. For me it was a delight to have any Muslim perspective represented in this publication and we went straight to work with our questions.

Our speaker on behalf of Islam was a Shia Muslim and practiced this since his birth. He was raised in a religious family as a Shia Muslim and studied Islam at Najaf in Iraq and Bahrain, in addition to his normal school education like any other growing child.

When asked how important is the spirit world in this belief system he replied,

'The spirit, the soul as referred to in the Quran, is very important.' Strangely though he saw the subjects of ghosts and related myths as, fictions and folkloric stories.

It should be noted that in the Qu'ran there are multiple worlds and life is scattered throughout. While we don't know specifically what this it may refer to the world of the "unseen" maybe hidden in there somewhere.

When quizzed about the soul and how it is view he stated, *'As Allah said in the holy Quran "They ask you about the Spirit, say: The Spirit is of the command of my Lord, the knowledge communicated to you is little." (verses 85 of chapter 17 of the holy book). Of course, The holy book talks about the soul, which perhaps doesn't differ very much from the world of the spirit, referred to by your question as the soul is on a journey specified in the Qu'ran that continues upon physical death'*

The question was asked if he believed in positive and negative influences within his belief system. He said that spirits are immobilized and they don't act, therefore, they make no influences. Spirits recognize are the souls and those influence the human being when he/she is alive. After death they become completely passive. However the Djinn are seen as inter dimensional beings that predate humanity. Like our Malaysian healer stated before it is believed where created by Allah, they have free will and can influence the living. Black magic is forbidden in Islam but maybe necessary to arrange a deal with the Djinn but its practice and can be severely punished, yet forms of it are practiced in various areas within the Muslim world.

In the Shia belief, the soul of the dead is said to return to hi or her house every Thursday night and watches what their sons are doing. He stated that the soul of the deceased rejoices when they witness them doing good things and suffers when they do wrong or bad things. But he went on to say that as spirits in the western sense don't exist then they cannot haunt the homes of other normal folks.

But this belief is not wide spread among the Sunnis because there is no Qu'ranic text alluding to this

However as our speaker insisted there was no spirits (those of humans) that could disturb a family home there never was an issue of a home becoming haunted by the spirits of the dead.

However Muslims around the world do a variety of things to rid the house of Djinn or bless the home upon moving in. The most obvious is Quranic readings.

These very spiritual cultures also engage in smudging by using various local materials and is done in the home while reciting certain verses from the Qu'ran.

Smudging within the west and other cultures could simply be the use of sage. Burning an amount of sage is seen to be the most potent destroyer of negativity and has been for centuries. The Muslim society also tend to mount certain verses from the Qu'ran in the home and was thought to keep out the Djinn or the evil eye which would be caused by Black Magic.

But should a Djinn become troublesome there are D jinn chasers in the Muslim world who deal with such issues however they are not found in all areas but can be found in Morocco, parts of Africa, and in Islamic areas of Southeast Asia as we discovered in Malaysia.

INDIA

Brief history of India, culture and religion

The first mainland Indian civilization arose in the Indus valley approximately 2,600 BC. However a more recent discovery off the west coast has revealed two cities under the ocean which has been carbon dated at around 12,000 BC. We have no idea whom these people where or what became of their fates, today the modern population of India reaches a vast 1,148 million.

The ever troublesome Europeans reached India by sea and the Portuguese began importing spices from India in 1498. The English got a foot hold and established the East India Company in 1600 to trade with India but by the 18th century the French and English became bitter rivals resulting in the 7 year war in 1756 and they both began to interfere in Indian politics.

With war raging the ruler of Bengal, Siraj-ud-Daula captured the British base at Calcutta and forced his captives into a small cell with most suffocating overnight and became known as the Black Hole of Calcutta within English terminology of the city.

In 1942 the National Congress demanded that the British quit India releasing control back to the Indian Hindu population. The British response was quick and jailed their leaders including the famous Gandhi who was freed again in 1944.

Hinduism is the major religion practiced in India by a massive 80% of the population whilst its close and controversial neighbour Pakistan is predominantly Muslim.

The Hindu Perspective

Devas we are told in the Hindu Scriptures when translated means 'The Shining ones' and are seen as heavenly beings. They are depicted in art and sculpture and are very visible throughout this continent depicted in sculptures on temple walls and forming wonderfully colourful statues on the temples roof top.

However there is a pecking order and Ishvara are seen as a supreme personal god and should not be mixed up with the Devas. The Indian epics speak of God materialising on earth in physical form to restore balance and dharma back into human culture in an attempt to lead them back Mosksha or Nirvana which is seen as the reunion with God.

Karma, a word surprisingly found its way into common English is a huge part of the Hindu belief system and when simply means an action, or work and refers to the law of cause and effect. The Hindu's believe that if we act and should cause a person harm or even think a harmful thought this will be re paid to us further down our life's path either in this life or the next as reincarnation is also a major factor in the belief system.

But unlike some sister beliefs in reincarnation the Hindu tradition believe we return as an animal and as such we should respect particular animals as they could be our ancestors. We are aware of a temple in India dedicated to rats and such like who are indeed treated like family and openly fed with chiefs slipping out dishes for thousands of rats that live inside the temple.

But for those that practice Hinduism the question is raised to their acceptance of spirits and of course troublesome spirits?

Christian traditions identify negative Demons, Muslim traditions identify the Jinn and of course the Hindu tradition identifies the Rakshasas. They are known for being a negative and unrighteous influence to anyone practicing this great religion.

In early Hindu traditions it was recognized and believed throughout various superstitions that the Rakshasas would often appear as lustful women who would lure men into

darkened areas and drink their blood. They were seen as having shape shifting abilities and took great delight in possessing vulnerable human hosts causing them to act similar to the Christian demons and commit acts of violence until the host is driven insane or ultimately death, a common trait still seen in Christianity and other sister beliefs.

It has been suggested the Rakshasas are powerful warrior type entities and can resort to the use of magic and illusion when unsuccessful with conventional weapons.

Their ability to change their appearances into various physical forms leaves it very unclear what their true form is. Interestingly like their close Demon and Jinn relations Rakshasas are capable of creating appearances which for those that try to dispel them would look successful, however in due course they can slip back and once again cause trouble.

In legends the Rakshasas where seen as cannibals, appearing on the battlefield when the death count was at its worst.

But we needed to learn more about this belief system and of course how they would deal with a situation with a spirit should one develop.

Most of us that find ourselves looking at the situation form a Christian aspect would consult a priest or minister or someone of similar rank to deal with the problem. However in the Hindu father this similar figure in the faith is known as a 'Pandit/Acharya' within the northern Areas of India whilst in the southern regions they would be known as a 'Purohit/Vadhyar'.

But getting inside the Hindi perspective was very difficult as the information is seen as being secret and it was difficult to get some of the information, but once again it was not impossible. Within the

Hindu religion as we touched already upon there are positive and negative powers identified and personal exorcism similar to other traditions is seen as being a necessary task if the person for instance is believed to be possessed by the spirit of an entity. Hindu's far and wide believe that following the death of a loved one their soul will hang around their possessions and other loved ones for up to one year. This in the western context of course seems a long time, but there are particular courses of action which must be adhered too and from what we learnt it seems some family members are responsible for mantra's which texts remain unknown to us which for most times are recited at the temple and are said for the soul of the deceased which makes it easier for them to travel onto their next path.

We can see in this part a huge difference in the involvement of the family to help their deceased relative than those of say the UK that tend to get back to normal living after about a week and by a year the deceased person has fallen to the back of their thoughts as we all are pushed into conformity by social and domestic pressures. But in the Hindu tradition it is seen that the responsibility to look after the soul of the deceased does not end once the person is buried. In many aspects within the west the very fact of addressing the soul does not even come into it. For the more stricter Hindu's it is important that the person should pass over lying flat on the ground and in contact with the earth.

Following the death it is customary that someone of the Hindu tradition be cremated rather than buried as it is seen as being one of the key factors which may lead to the development of a haunting as the deceased display their displeasure. Burning the body is seen as a way of releasing the soul as the flames represent the presence of their God Brahma and as reincarnation is a key factor in their belief the funeral is seen more as a celebration than of funeral in the western concept.

Following the cremation this time of mantra recital at the temple is an opportunity for those that may have done some wrong to the deceased person the ability to express their sorrow for what they did to the deceased person and apologize.

It seems that the event of death is not the end within Hindu tradition and following those set parameters and understanding for the deceased can help in preventing the haunting from occurring as it falls heavily onto the family not to be forgot those that have past.

Following the various prayers and mantra's from friends and family it is said that after one year the ashes of the deceased is brought to the sea or river and dissolved.

Once this is done a small silver likeness of the deceased is taken the temple and the soul is allowed to travel onto their next level. It is a traditional belief within the Hindu culture for the soul to leave this body and move onto the next on its journey to its ultimate goal of Nirvana.

So once again we see that daily or weekly remembrance of the deceased is in its own way could be a preventive measure for haunting's to even begin. How many of us move into properties where previous owners haven past away and we don't even shed them a thought, not even to light a candle in their remembrance?

Selling your soul

There are many other ways of removing spirit which would take the person on a darker path and these various paths we would not recommend. Barry was first introduced to Jadoo, a form of black magic by a book written by the late John A Keel appropriately named Jadoo. The book was an account of John's travels around the world and of course into the Middle East including India and Tibet where he was first introduced to the phenomenon of Jadoo.

Jadoo was and is a system of magic seen as being quite hazardous to those involved or those targeted by this type of black magic. One online account of a person diagnosed with being the victim of Jadoo resulted in a very deep rooted superstition as the responses to his plea for help seemed to indicate.

Although there was no sign as to how the diagnosis was carried out on the victim whom we shall call Aban, he went on to explain that the only way he could be freed from such a curse was to allow the Jadoo priest who diagnosed him in the first place to slaughter several dozen sheep and just over half a dozen black fowls, of course providing a payment was made for the service, I wonder did he accept credit cards.

A host of these tales can be found in the areas where Jadoo has a fixed hold on the cultures imagination and it has been suggested that those that practice Jadoo do so with the aid of the shayateen, a demon recognized in the Middle East. In some teachings of the Quran in modern day Iraq and state tell a story that some of the shayateen climbed up on each others shoulders until they could reach the lowest levels of the heavens, where they could hear the Angels.
It was believed from this act they could briefly gain some little knowledge, and then pass this knowledge on to those willing to listen such as psychics and mediums and the reason sometimes the mediums were right.
But of course it is also stated that the information can be haphazard as the shayateen themselves only learn a few things from what they overhear.
Jadoo from what we can gain is of course an avenue which may offer some relief from a haunting but one we would advise not to follow.

Accounts from Pakistan indicate just how dark the practice can be. We must remember Pakistan is indeed a proud Muslim country yet this practice of black magic has been insidious, creeping into all walks of life within the country and has been seen from various people on the ground within Pakistan to be a growing threat.

On Jan 11th 2010 a disturbing account of Kala Jadoo was reported from Korangi, an area in Karachi. It was stated that during a form of exorcism the priest cut the throat of his four year old daughter and her remains where buried in the rear of the property. It was the diligence of a neighbor who raised the alarm and her remains where uncovered.

There is always a darker path, in every society, in every belief but we implore the reader not to follow this path and stay to the light.

Tread Softly

Tread softly around my birth and name,
For my life was long and bitter.
Weeds and long ago dead flowers,
Surround me as memories liter.

My silent neighbors like me,
Were forgotten long ago.
Moments of regret, the aging years,
No longer to be our foe.

Memories of tears that seemed,
To heal the inner soul.
Tears that were not seen by me,
Until I was placed below.

Kindly donated to this publication from 'Inner Silence', a collection of poems by Tearah.

Personal Remarks

In conclusion for Dustin and I to bring you some solutions from different cultures and belief systems from around the world has been a great pleasure.

For those that have found themselves the victims of a negative haunting we do hope you find some solace in these pages.

But one thing that was very apparent to both of us during our time in Asia was the huge difference in spiritual remembrance and the lack of this in the western cultures. I have started to address this issue myself within my own views and daily life and has brought me great happiness and I hope to those that have gone before me.

Barry FitzGerald

Personal Remarks

I would just once again like to stress my main reason for being involved in this field, which is to shed some light on the existence of the afterlife. Not to prove or disprove any specific religion, but solely to bring forth a greater understanding of how we are all connected in this world and how each of our actions, no matter how mundane,

affects the lives of others, generations to come, and the very fabric of the Universe.

It is my hope that by making people aware of an existence beyond this one, we will as a society become less self-centered and self focused; that we will learn to live for the greater good, to take care of one other, and treat everyone with the kindness, compassion, and respect that we all deserve.

In the end, I am just trying to do my part to fix the world, one act of kindness at a time.
Thanks for reading -- Tikkun Olam for life.

Dustin J. Pari

ISBN 978-1-4478-6528-5